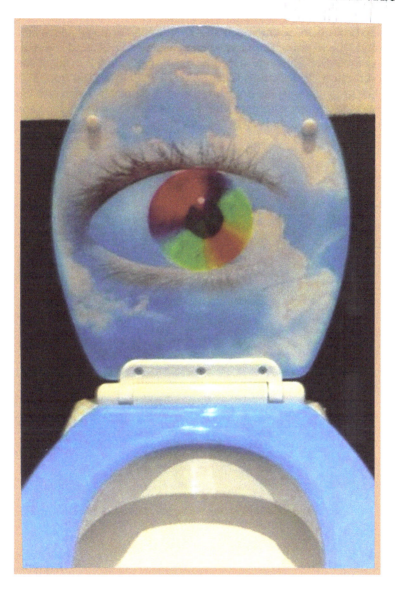

The Ladies: picture taken by IB at The Den, Harrogate

Don't flush your dreams
down the toilet

About the author

Ida Barker spent seven dedicated years (2003 - 2010) busking her self-penned songs on Bridlington, Scarborough and York streets, to gigging pubs and clubs in and around the **North of England**, gaining airplay on BBC Radio York and BBC Radio Humberside. A change is as good as a reply, with this in mind, she chose a **new direction** - to become a fiction writer (pseudonym **Zizzi Bonah**). In memory to her late grandparents, Ida Bona and Thomas Bateman-Hullah who farmed within Nidderdale, the author's **nom de plume** came about - merging Bona and Hullah into Bonah

==> ida performing on stage at
The Boardwalk, Sheffield 2008
Picture taken by Ian Parker

Hole Bottom Farms
Dacre, Harrogate, West Riding of Yorkshire
(when county boarders changed this became North Yorkshire)

==>
Tommy & Ida Hullah's
wedding day 1931

Tommy and Ida Hullah owned and farmed Hole Bottom Farms for many years. They were shorthorn dairy farmers with sidelines of breeding large whites, sheep and free-range poultry

Mum, Daughter &
Moggy the cat

In 2016 Mother and Daughter - Gwen Hullah and Ida Barker, set up in partnership a **book publishing** business, aptly called **She And The Cat's Mother**. **All in-house**, complete format: writing, editing, proof reading, formatting paperbacks and eBooks, to raising profile on social media - the only tasking they have not done is the printing. The acid test is getting their books into the highway of readers' minds. They are authorpreneurs!

#GirlLikeYou

How to **format** your script, play, musical, novel or poetry & self-publish to paperback & eBook

written by **Ida Barker**
edited by Gwen Hullah

She And The Cat's Mother

Published by She And The Cat's Mother 2018

SheAndTheCatsMother.co.uk

Copyright Ida Barker 2018
All rights reserved
IdaBarker.com

GirlLikeYou.online

Photographs courtesy of the author

Printed by IngramSpark

A CIP catalogue record for this book is available from the British Library

Paperback ISBN: 9780995747968
eBook ISBN: 9780995747999

Cover and interior design by She And The Cat's Mother

Dedication
With love and thanks to Gwen Hullah (my mother) for reading the typescript and suggesting alterations and additions

Dear reader,

Enhance chance

While others have dreamt about writing a book, you
have written one. The next hurdle? Getting it out
there, on sale. This able to enable manual, will
show you how to format your self-published book,
ensuring it is compatible with all retailers and
distributors within one week. It will save you time
and money; ideal for shoe-string budgets

Mirror-me tech

Take new heart, while self-publishing your book will
be a technical process, you do not need to be an
academic or a HTML computer programmer. I started
out with no programming skills, but with sheer
bloody-mindedness, (aided by search engine Google),
I can honestly say, I taught myself whilst working
going-along-to-get-along jobs - I've done the hard
work, so you don't have to. By the time you turn the
final page of this manual, you will be able to say,
'I did it. You can too!'

Bright now

There is no better time than now - you have asked
the ask, now do the do - empower yourself by taking
charge of your creative works and self-publish your
book today!

Ida Barker
#GirlLikeYou

Contents

Formatting

Quotes of encouragement

Fall in and follow me
Read the Novishiat recipe
page 9

Piers Morgan's note of reply
page 194

The 12 Commandments of an Authorpreneur "Thou shalt NOT ..."

Inspiration
Harrogate
Tour de France
sculpture
page 178

Blogs (as posted on zizziology.com)

Note to reader:
At the beginning of each formatting chapter is a quote of encouragement, and at the end is a blog of interest from zizziology.com; followed by 1 of the 12 commandments of an authorpreneur

Foreword Welcome

Action: You made an investment of money when you bought this insightful self-publishing manual. Do NOT wait for someone other to do the work or the choosing for you. Be yourself. More like yourself - ignore discouraging sources who say "You can't have everything" but you sometimes can!

Vision: It all boils down to how much do you want to see your stories in print? Then, if your book turns out to be scimpier than you had envisaged - do not be like the Lapwing trailing her wings - remember - Yorkshire folk serve Yorkshire pudding with thick, beef gravy as a separate course before the "Roast" to fill-up the intermittent gap of the avid meat-eaters' appetite. This is not prudence, continuity is vital

Dedication: And there is nothing quite like self-learning to shape the mind. It offers scope and the distinct feelings of freedom and great expectations; plus by embracing these prowess directions, a girl (or guy) like you, will avoid the "razor blades" of modern techicalities with creditable valour - as one academic lady said: "Such different people."

Shrewdness: Inherent tight fistedness without letting it show is not meanness. It is a means to an end through self-reliance, working within a slender income. Tersely, another source remarked: "It's cash-strapped characters like these who entertain without having the expense of guests."

Flair: It is magical when your words dance perfectly together, but remember - readers do love a bitch in every story ... According to an inside source who does not want to be named either - recalled: The bachelor farm-man who invited a long-lost friend to a fish and chip supper. During the mealtime the guest noticed often - the border collie bitch sagaciously watching every mouthful of food he eat. Eventually he asked, "Why the fixed stare?" "Oh, take no notice of old lassie," the other replied. "You're eating off her plate."

Absolution: Sincerely, there are no mindfields to trip you up within this manual, and almost most of the unending successions; of almost insoluble - insomnia - problems have been painstakingly worked out and put into practice. So no salty tears, only the leak of happiness, for a girl (or guy) like you!

Good luck
Gwen Hullah

Fall in and follow me

The Novishiat recipe

1kg (2lb) action
400g (1lb) vision
300g (12oz) dedication
200g (8oz) shrewdness
100g (4oz) flair
50g (2oz) absolution
25g (1oz) luck

Method:

Mix together, action, vision, and dedication
until well blended. Add shrewdness while stirring
in flair with generousity. Fold in absolution -
do not beat - or ingenuity could curdle

Continue stirring while adding flavours of love,
hate, resolution, with the essence of free-guilt

Whisk out seeds of doubt. Replace them with the
power of intention

Sweeten with extracts from flowers of fine
thoughts and the sauce of good luck

Recipe created by GH

Girl

Like

You

1

Be yourself;
everyone else is already taken

- Oscar Wilde
writer

IB's certificate of merit: Pianoforte Solo - Beginners

A combination of hardwork, creativity and self-determination and things start to take shape

Essentials:
The right computer
software

Why Listen to Me?

My intention writing #GirlLikeYou, is to provide you with the kind of manual that had not been written when I sort a path to self-publishing. Through frustration, unable to find and follow one spokesperson to show the way, I Googled every step, researching different techniques, for different systems, by different people. I know the struggle. It took years of:

.Self-education
It is not enough being a writer, you must learn new skills: how to create your brand, and how to sustain a social media presence without just saying 'buy my book'

.Penny-pinching
Seeking access to industry magazines without paying a personal fortune in subscription, I gained employment at a high-street bookshop

.Fine-tuning
I spent hours looking at YouTube videos learning how to fill out a tax return, and how to present a typed script to industry standards, invaluable knowledge I would never have had access to without meeting the right people – but taken with a grain of sea salt, never lose your enthusiasm to change and fine-tune in order to grow

As every #GirlLikeYou knows, start with the end in mind, and you bypass the fun along the way

With all this in mind, I would like to think I know my readers, because I am a #GirlLikeYou

The Power of Intention

Bred by my northern parents – whose roots go back hundreds of years to Yorkshire – I was instilled with a can-do approach. Mother, a farmer's daughter, founded and later managed Radio Witham (1975 – 1987), this meant, from the age of four I loved a range of music, from Boy George, Shakin' Stevens, Fats Domino, to Dr Hook & the Medicine Show – these influences led to piano lessons. Sometimes we all need a nod or a nudge in a certain direction to help us succeed at a task

From Me to You

Here is your nod/nudge in the right direction – you are going to need the following software to fulfil every step in this book:

> Microsoft Word to structure your manuscript and paperback interior layout (FREE trial for 30 days)

> Adobe Photoshop to design your cover (FREE trial for 30 days)

> Adobe Acrobat Pro to generate a PDF for your print-ready cover and interior (FREE trial for 30 days)

> Notepad++ to format your eBook (FREE forever)

> Calibre to convert your eBook to an ePub file – making it ready for distributors to market (FREE forever)

I.A – Essentials: The right computer software

Memorida: Different software versions –

If you have the software recommended in this book, or are purchasing the software for the first time, you may have different versions than those used in my examples. Do not be discouraged #GirlLikeYou! Simply click F1 on your keyboard for Help. Alternatively ask Google – everything I know about self-publishing has been learnt from trial and error and searching the world wide web

Note-This: All computer commands in this book refer to those on a PC – for Mac commands go to Google. PLEASE DO deface this manual. It is a working guidebook. Add to it, cross things out, write down ideas and inspiration in "Your Notes" section towards the back pages of the paperback edition

With a raft of optimism

Picture: Radio Witham receive cheque (1976)

As reported in the Grantham Journal: Helping "Radio Witham" a broadcasting service for Grantham Hospital patients, on its way. Officer Commanding R.A.F. Swinderby, Group Capt. D. Green, third from the left, hands a cheque for £164, raised by his men, to Mr R. Keightley, on behalf of the Friends of Grantham Hospital. Also in the picture, from the left, are Flt. Lieut. Ben Theed, Barry Mac, David Wood, Tessa Wood, Gwen Barker (nee Hullah) and Garry Wakefield

B
L
O
G

Bear's retreat

How to increase your chances to write daily

Bear-faced

There is a saying: "**When eating alfresco with friends and savaged by a hungry bear, all you need to do to survive is outrun one of your friends, not the bear!**" Which made me think ...

How can we create better chances to write daily?

There is a **general guide** by many writers that between 1,000 to 2,000 words should be written daily. But how realistic is this? Noting when we fall behind, we are often discouraged to write tomorrow

I find it better to set a lower word count, one that is far easier to reach and often surpass - **generating enthusiasm to write daily** - whether it be 50, 100, 200 words

Remember, you don't need to outrun the bear

The 12 COMMANDMENTS of an AUTHORPRENEUR

Giveaways

#1

Thou shalt NOT

undervalue one's writing by giving it away for free

Just spreading the word ...

IB at Surf & Sea sports bar, Malta

*You've read Chapter 1, now
let's move to the next level*

2

Perception is everything
The skill is making it the truth

- Female Munrah, fictional character in book,
#Entrangement: Where Colours Don't Bleed
by ZB

"

Chair with flower cushion: picture by IB at Chelsea Flower Show 2013, London

Plant yourself on a comfy seat before reading the following Chapter

Prepare your manuscript in Microsoft Word

The 90/10 Ratio = Magic!

You may have heard the expression:

> *'To succeed in anything it takes 90 per cent preparation and 10 per cent per luck'*

The importance of preparing should not be over-looked, neither should it be skimped. And, while you may think your manuscript is hunky-dory-bound-for-glory, once you begin commanding Word to do tasks, surprisal things may arise. For example, if you have used tabs or spaces at the start of your paragraphs instead of indents, you are going to find formatting problems later

Step 1 – Important!
Back-up Always Stacks-up:

Save a copy of your manuscript in case you make a lasting mistake

Step 2 –
Use the Blitz Method to Remove Bad Formatting

The Blitz Method will ensure your manuscript does not contain hidden errors which can arise if it has been transferred from other programmes, or if it began as a PDF and later converted to Word. To achieve the Blitz Method you will need to access your computer's text editor such as Windows Notepad (TextEditor for Mac)

Memorida: How do I locate Windows Notepad? – Go to Programs: Accessories, or use the search box in File Explorer and type in: Windows Notepad

Ready #GirlLikeYou? Then let's start the Blitz Method:

> Open the file containing your manuscript
> Press Ctrl + A (hold Ctrl key, then press A key at same time) this will highlight your entire manuscript
> Press Ctrl + C to copy your manuscript
> Open Windows Notepad
> Press Ctrl + V to paste your manuscript into Windows Notepad

Instantly, your manuscript will have a different – more plainer look about it as all the formatting has been stripped from your text

> If you copied your manuscript from Microsoft Word, close Word
> Open (or Reopen) Word for a fresh empty document
> Return to Windows Notepad:
> Press Ctrl + A to highlight your entire manuscript (see picture II.A)

The Notepad window shows:

```
SALT

#Salt - Sensing I am alone now, I open my eyes and confirm there is nothing between myself and the flickering sou
Moments ago, a prison guard hurled the book into my cell - taunting words followed - according to common wisdom
I lower the book, letting the candlelight shine onto it. The title reads: Prisoner Of The Past: Salt Delray. I op
I take the candle and move it close to the book. The hot wax drips onto the pages, the liquid runs, spelling out
Turning my face to the wall, despair escapes me which isn't silent. I only hope my instincts aren't as close as
But if I'm wrong?
The cell door bangs open. I wheel round. A prison guard rasps, "It's time!"

(1) PITCH WHITE

#WaterHasAMemory - His cold steely eyes reflected only the face that looked into them. Her face.
She barely recognised herself. Her naturally illustrious cinnamon-black hair hung shamefully damp and lank, plac
"Salt Delray," he began. "Under the law of Supreme Munrah, you have been found guilty of murder by drowning Kielf
Salt felt like someone who had been struck without warning. Engaging in reflection that gave back dullness and w
Judge Helsby's voice continued to grate like granite across the courtroom. "To prepare leaving the fourth element
Lowering his reflective eyes and with commanding weight, he bought down the gavel. "Guards! Pursue the Metalgant
Forcibly, two Metalgant prison guards who had shadowed Salt since her arrest, directed her through an ornate door
Devastated, through word of mind, Salt spoke to Rhuand - The fault didn't lie in the loving, but in the circumst
Her shackled departure echoed loudly down passageway after passageway, but Salt didn't protest. Now now. She kne
Salt needed time to think -
Could there be a way out?
She recognised there was little food or sympathy from Metalgant prison guards. And less so now she had been convi
Bang!
The guards slammed shut the reinforced iron clad door behind her with menacing force, then lifted up the lozenge-
"Occupancy of prisoner Delray resumed!" jeered prison guard one, the taller of the two men. She closed harasssed
"Yeah, innocent, eh?" taunted the other. "She may as well plead the rain's snowing fast."
```

II.A – Opening paragraphs of novel #Entrangement

> Press Ctrl + C to copy

> Go to new document in Word

> Press Ctrl + V to paste contents of Notepad document into Word

> Go to File in Word and Save your Word document as a .doc file
   (I always choose "Word 97-2003 Document")

> Close Notepad (no need to save)

Now #GirlLikeYou we can start formatting!!

Step 3 –

View your New Format in Word:

> Press (Ctrl + Shift + 8)

> All formatting marks will now be visible; paragraphs and spaces (see picture II.B)

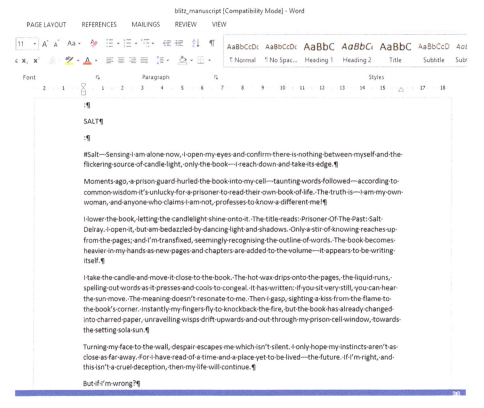

II.B – Opening paragraphs of novel #Entrangement

Memorida: Where's my italics gone? –

You will notice all your italics, bold and underlined fonts have been cleaned away through the Blitz Method – this was necessary – you will reinstate them in a later Chapter

Step 4 –

Remove Double Spaces after Full Stops:

> Select All (Ctrl + A)

> Activate the Find and Replace box (Ctrl + H)

> Type two spaces in Find section; one space in Replace section

> Click Replace All

Step 5 –

Clean up any Extra Space at the End of Paragraphs:

> Ensure Find and Replace box is open

> Replace .[space]^p with .^p and they will vanish

Note-This: Do not type [space] but press your spacebar [ ]

Step 6 –

At the Beginning of Each Paragraph – Spaces Instead of Indents?:

> Select All (Ctrl + A)

> Open Find and Replace box (Ctrl + H)

> Place cursor in Find section, then click More (bottom left)

> Click Special and select Tab Character

> Leave Replace section empty

> Click Replace All

Memorida: Varied space –

If you used spaces for indents, key in the number of spaces you used into Find section. Do this a number of times if your spaces vary

Step 7 –

Apply Normal Paragraph Style to Whole Body of your Text

What are Styles? –

Here, we do not need to bring to mind the singer Harry Styles, nor should we reminisce about bad-hairstyles, but to be precise, Paragraph Styles. They allow you to uniformly control the styling of your book by applying different Styles to different features. You need only change the Style once and this will have a ripple effect across your entire book. Exciting!!

Memorida: The best way forward –

It is easiest to start with Normal Style and unify the entire manuscript as the majority of your book will

need indented paragraphs, later you will create
your own custom Styles for different features such
as headings, copyright page and first paragraphs
without indents (in the case of novels)

Let's begin:

> Select All (Ctrl + A)

> Press Alt + Ctrl + Shift + S (or Home tab; click Styles arrow – II.C)

II.C

> A selection of Styles to choose from will appear

> Hover your cursor over Normal

> Click on the arrow next to Normal, or right click your mouse

> You will see a drop down menu

> Select Modify (see picture II.D) and the Modify box will open

If you want to change the default Style:

> Click Format (bottom left)

> Click Font (see picture II.E)

A new pop-up box will appear:

> Select the font and size (see picture II.F)

> Click OK

II.D

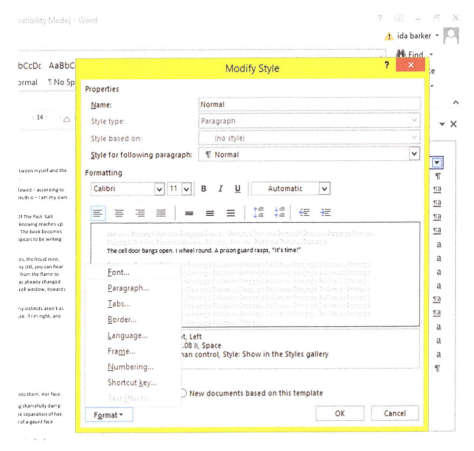

II.E

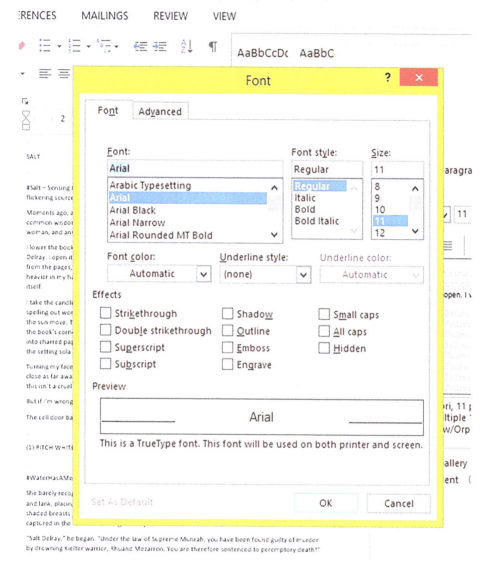

II.F

Now lets explore the differences for Normal Styles regarding a Script, Play, Musical, Novel and Poetry – MEMO: above each of the Paragraph pop-up boxes in the next four pictures, you can see which font and size of font I have selected!!

SCREENPLAYS: Film and TV mostly have paragraphs with indents either side of speech, therefore:

> Go to Format, Click Paragraph; Go to Indents And Spacing

> For General, Alignment: Left

> For Indentation, select Left 1.81 cm, Right 1.61 cm

> In Special, select First Line

> Enter a dimension in By, 0.01 cm

> Select Line Spacing, i.e. 1.5 lines

> Click OK (see picture II.G)

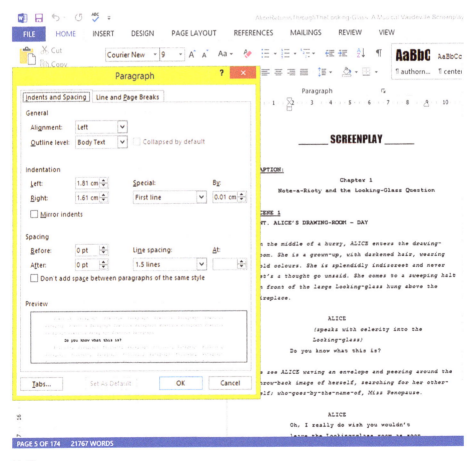

II.G

PLAYS mostly have speech paragraphs that hang: first line looks normal, but other lines below have an indent on left side (see preview box inside picture II.H) therefore:

> Go to Format; Click Paragraph; Go to Indents And Spacing

> For General, Alignment: Left

> In Special, select Hanging

> Enter a dimension in By, 1.3 cm

> Select Line Spacing, i.e. 1.5 lines

> Click OK (see picture II.H)

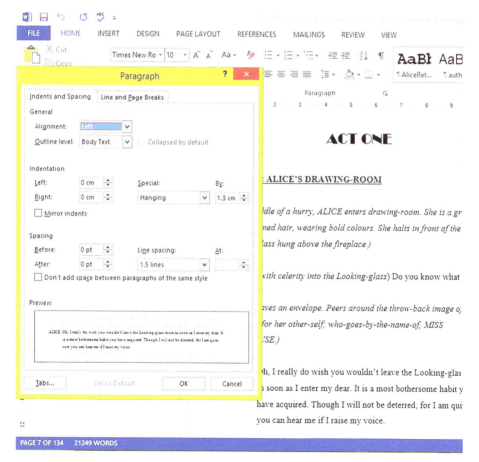

II.H

NOVELS mostly have paragraphs with indents that go in by a space measurement of four or five letters, therefore:

> Go to Format; Click Paragraph; Go to Indents And Spacing

> For General, Alignment: Left

> Go to Special

> Select First Line

> Enter a dimension in By, i.e. 0.76 cm or 0.79 cm

> While you are here select your Line Spacing, i.e. 1.5 lines

> Click OK (see picture II.I)

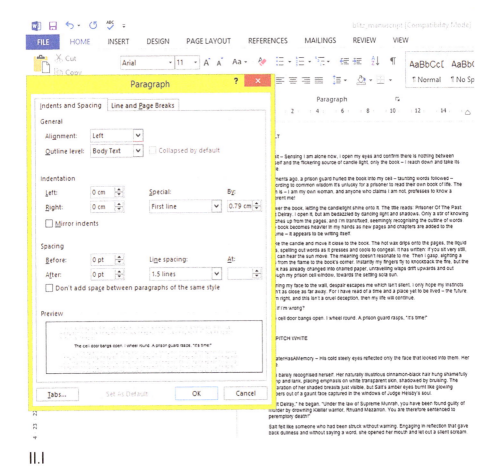

II.I

POETRY mostly has centered paragraphs, therefore:

> Go to Format; Click Paragraph; Go to Indents And Spacing

> For General, Alignment: Centered

> In Special, select (none)

> Select Line Spacing, i.e. 1.5 lines

> Click OK (see picture II.J)

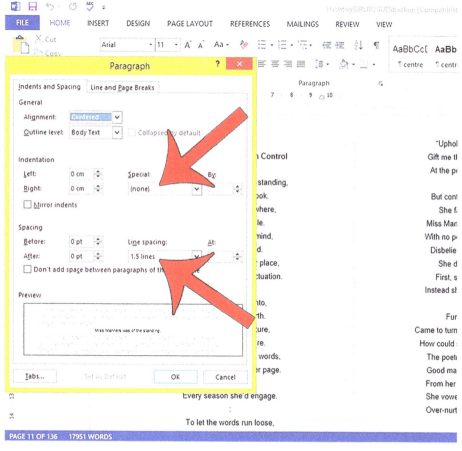

II.J

Within Chapter 4: Format Your Paperback Interior, you will create other Paragraph Styles for your work that are different to Normal within your script, play, musical, novel or poetry

Memorida: Stylistics for Musicals –

All Musicals are formatted as a Film/TV Script or

Play, we will look at the presentation of song lyrics

in Chapter 4

Note-This: You do not have to consistently follow my dimensions when it comes to the design of your manuscript, but by following my Steps, you will know how to alter the text layout for your preferred look. Also worth mentioning: if choosing different height/width of paperback, and/or different fonts and sizes to the ones I use, you may need to tweak Styles. For example, formatting a screenplay – basic rule: look at the proportions, try to mimic them

Step 8 –

Disable Automatic Numbering or Bullet Points, and Insert Numbers and Lists Manually:

> Click File or Microsoft Office button (top left of your screen)

> Click Word Options (see picture II.K)

> Click Proofing

> Click AutoCorrect Options (see picture II.L)

> Click AutoFormat As You Type tab (see picture II.M)

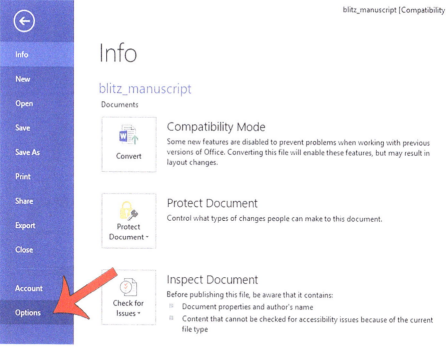

II.K

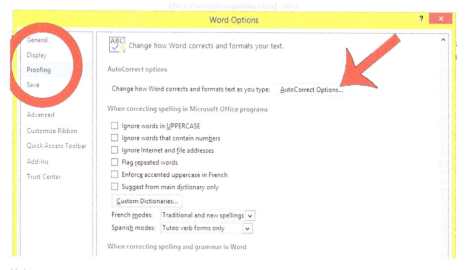

II.L

47

II.M

> Under Apply As You Type, clear Automatic Bulleted Lists tick box

> And clear the Automatic Numbered Lists tick box

> Click OK

Take care with a dinosaur called Thesaurus, as mentioned in ZB's book,
Alice Returns Through The Looking-Glass, extract below:

"Now, whatever you do, do not wake the Thesaurus too often. For if you ride the Thesaurus too far through your story, you shall simply wear him out. And while I cannot afford to buy another Thesaurus, I can afford to buy another writer!"

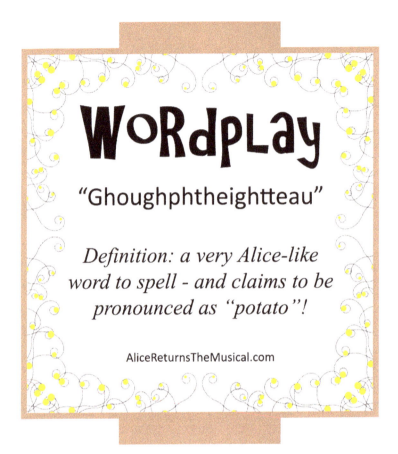

WoRdpLay

"Ghoughphtheightteau"

Definition: a very Alice-like word to spell - and claims to be pronounced as "potato"!

AliceReturnsTheMusical.com

Here is how:
gh stands for p (as the last letters in hiccough);
ough for o (as in dough);
phth stands for t (as in phthisic);
eigh stands for a (as in neighbour);
tt stands for t (as in gazette);
and eau stands for o (as in beau)!

B
L
O
G

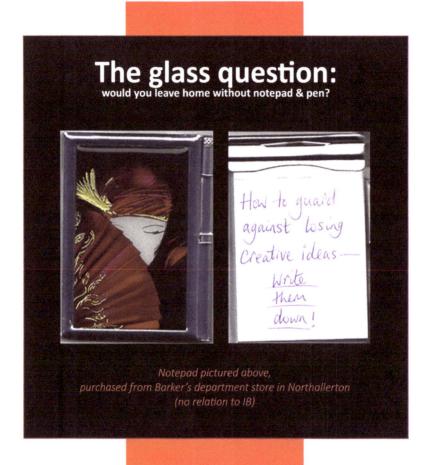

The glass question:
would you leave home without notepad & pen?

How to guard
against losing
creative ideas—
Write
them
down!

Notepad pictured above,
purchased from Barker's department store in Northallerton
(no relation to IB)

The glass question and how to guard against losing creative ideas

You overhear a phrase or an observation that you just know will fit seamlessly into your creative writing - **the glass question is**: will you remember it by the time you reach your manuscript?

Often the answer is no

Solution: don't leave home without a notepad and pen!

Author Jilly Cooper famously would take pen and paper to all her dinner parties and events, writing down the audible, lord-able gems from her guests' conversations. Amazingly her guests never took offence, in fact, they played up to these occasions, then waited impatiently for her next book in the hope they would recognise themselves amongst her carefully crafted characters

Take note: guard against the glass question

The 12 COMMANDMENTS of an AUTHORPRENEUR

Merchandise

#2

Thou shalt NOT

wear one's own merchandise
in a bid to encourage others
to buy it

IB wearing "Miss Manners & Mirth Control" t-shirt - Malta

Who else will wear it - if not me, me, me?

Why not declare allegiance to Zizzi's fantasy characters by putting on the
Raz-Rez - purchases can be made from zazzle.co.uk/zizzibonah

Published on Saturday
10 February 2018
within
The Yorkshire Post,
Gwen Hullah's
Letter-to-the-Editor
regarding: Memories
of Hannah Hauxwell
was included

The Yorkshire Post; Harrogate Advertiser

There's more than one write way:
Try your local newspapers and
listing pages

3

Be like a duck. Calm on the surface,
but always paddling like the dickens
underneath

- Sir Michael Caine CBE
actor

Dragons: picture taken by IB at Chelsea Flower Show 2013, London

Dragons represent good fortune
in Chinese Astrology

Design your eBook cover

The Time is Now o'Clock

"What? So soon!" I hear you say. "Well, time is the footsteps that nobody can hear," is my reply

You are going to design your eBook cover as soon as now for one good reason: you need to know what style of writing fonts you are going to use on your book cover – as the same fonts will be used inside your book for both the title page and the headings – enabling you to have a more professional look

Memorida: Colour pallet –

The range of colours you choose for your text (book title, author name) should be colours already shown within the cover image itself, this makes for a quality look

Memorida: Let it breathe –

Keep your cover uncluttered; if you choose a busy image you may struggle to find enough space for your text. Remember: space allows the eye to move around better. Think big, bold, beautiful

Step 1 –

Download the eBook Cover Template

> Go to GirlLikeYou.online/self-publish-your-book-templates.html

> Key in this password to gain access: GLY665463

> Save the .psd file to your chosen location

> Open the .psd file

> If you see a message that fonts are missing, ignore this

> Alternatively, you might receive a message asking if you would like to "Create New Library", click cancel for now (see picture III.A)

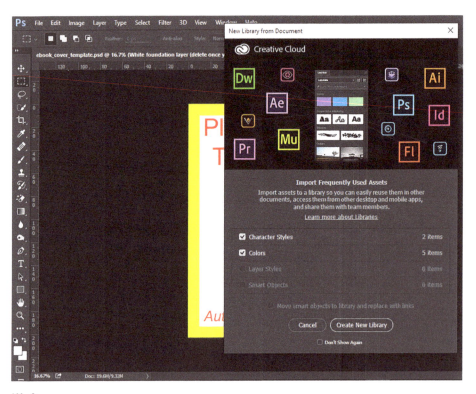

III.A

> Click File

> Save As, renaming this file as your own book cover

Step 2 –

Summarising the Open eBook Cover Template:

> You will see there is a good amount of space around the yellow margins free from text – this forward thinking will cause no hold-ups when you transfer your design onto the paperback template

> I have chosen an easy-on-the-eye font to cover many genres, but choose one from the drop down menu if it suits you better (instructions listed in Step 6 of this Chapter) – or download free ones from Google

Step 3 –

Choosing an Image for your eBook Cover:

You can either:

> Upload a photo taken by yourself, or

> If you are already creative with Photoshop then design one, or

> Buy an affordable image from Shutterstock.com, or

> Search for copyright-free images by surfing the internet

The image you chose to use within your eBook cover must have a minimum of 300 DPI resolution (preferably 350 DPI)

Ensure you have already viewed your selected image in Photoshop before inserting it into your template, and check the DPI by:

> Selecting Image in horizontal Tool Bar

> Choose Image Size (see picture III.B)

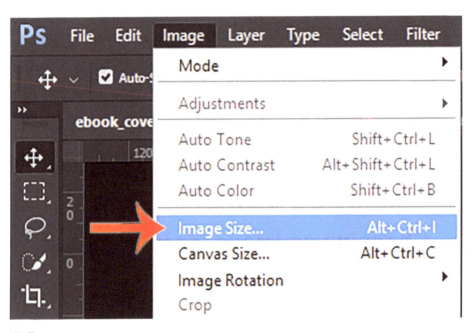

III.B

> The Image Size pop-up box will appear (see picture III.C)

> Insert "350" into resolution box

> Click OK

III.C

Step 4 –

Inserting the Image for your eBook:

Whilst viewing your eBook cover template within Photoshop, ensure the layers panel is open – located at the right hand side of your screen (if not, click the F7 key "or" click Windows button on your keyboard, plus the F7 key)

Now, referencing picture III.D, note the red arrow is pointing to the "White foundation layer" within the layers panel – this layer needs to be highlighted before inserting your eBook image

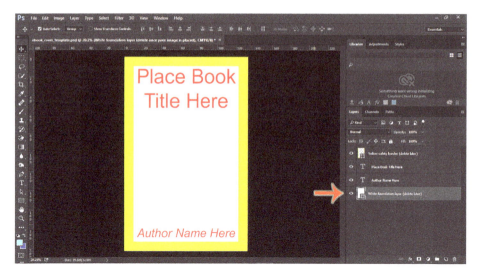

III.D

Click your mouse over the layer and it will change to a lighter grey

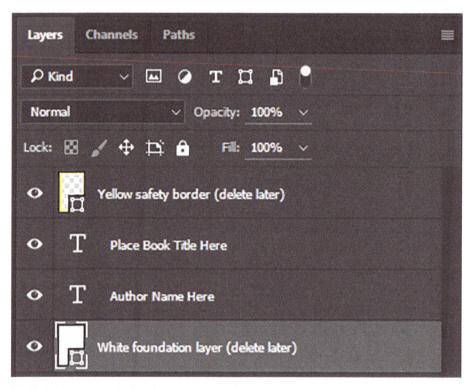

III.E (close-up of the layers panel)

To insert your own image:

> Go to File

> Choose Place Embedded or Place (picture III.F)

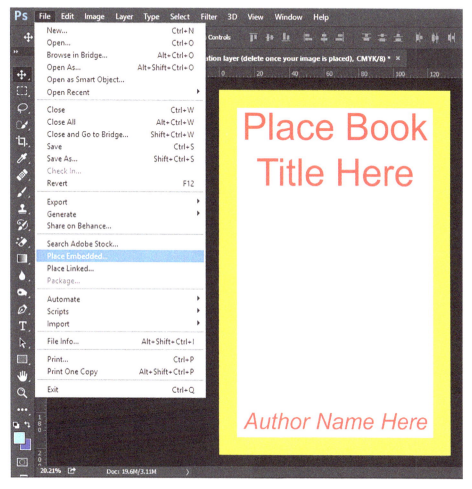

III.F

> A pop up box will appear

> Search for the image you want from your computer

> Click Place (see picture III.G for an example of a file to be placed)

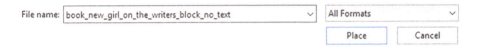

File name: book_new_girl_on_the_writers_block_no_text   All Formats

Place   Cancel

III.G

> Click the Maintain Aspect Ratio button (see picture III.H) this will ensure the proportions of your image are not distorted

III.H

Once activated: Ratio button will be highlighted (see picture III.I)

III.I

> Drag the edges of your image so that it does not fall short of the yellow margins, but covers the full 5.25 inches width x 8 inches height behind the yellow margins

Now:

> Click on the Move Tool, or press V on your keyboard to highlight it (see picture III.J) this will activate the placement of your image

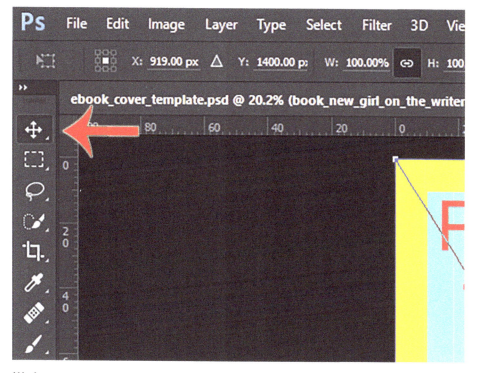

III.J

A pop-up box will now be visible, containing the message to place the image (see picture III.K)

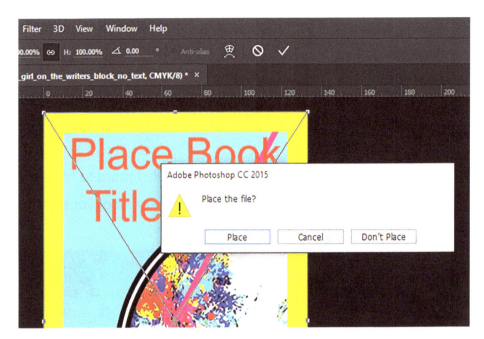

III.K

> Click Place

Step 5 –

Ensure No Text goes into Trim Areas

The best way to do this, is to have the Yellow margin at the forefront of all other layers within the layers panel. If it becomes hidden from sight, at the back of other layers, then:

> Go to layers panel

> Click on the Yellow Safety Border layer

> In horizontal Tool Bar, select Layers

> Select Bring To Front (see picture III.L)

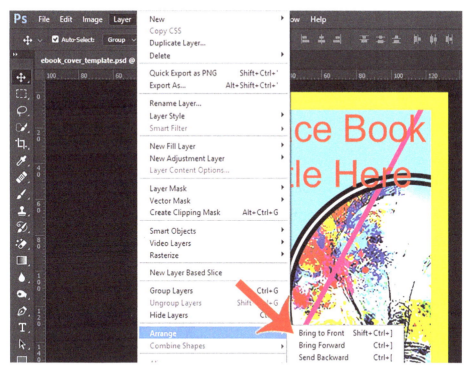

III.L

Memorida: Yellow Safety Border (margin) –
This will be deleted later, and is NOT part of your
design

Step 6 –
Inserting your Book Title onto Template:

> Press T on your keyboard

> You will see highlighted the T in vertical Tool Bar to the left (see picture III.M)

73

III.M

> Click cursor on PLACE BOOK TITLE HERE

> Press Ctrl + A to choose all text – the words are now highlighted
  (see picture III.N)

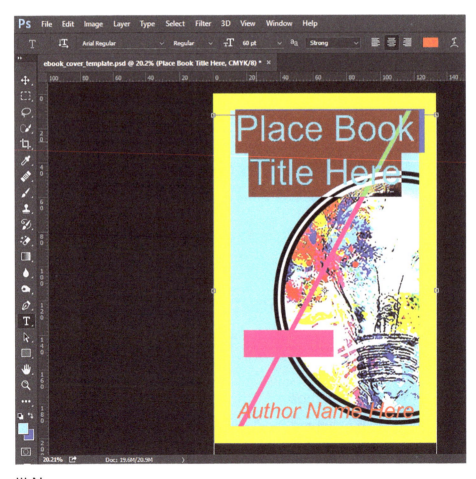

III.N

> Pick your favoured style of font (lettering) by clicking on the drop-down font menu (see picture III.O)

III.O

> Make your selection from the vast choice of fonts (see picture III.P)

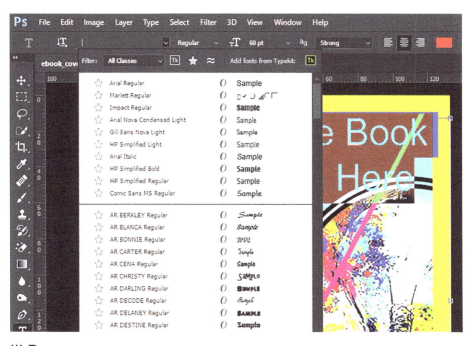

III.P

> While text is still highlighted, type in your book title

Note-This: If text goes into yellow margin – adjust text size, (and for other adjustments, like space set between each letter) simply:

> Click "Toggle Character and Paragraph panels" (picture III.Q)

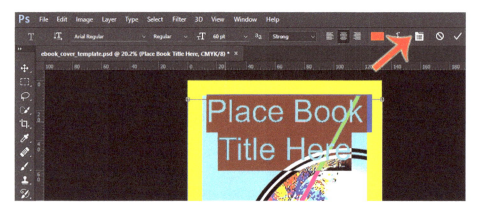

III.Q

> The Character panel appears first (circled in red; see picture III.R)

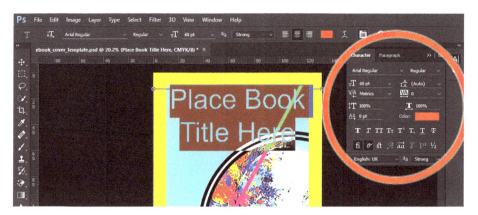

III.R

> To open the Paragraph panel, click on Paragraph (see III.S)

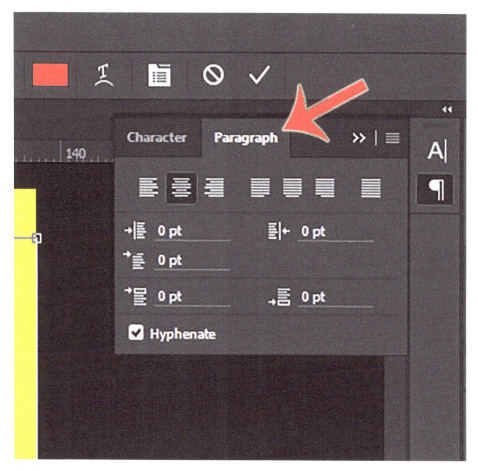

III.S

Note-This: Before closing the Character and Paragraph panels, follow Step 7 of this Chapter

Step 7 –

Select a Colour for Book Title from Colours within your Image

Whilst in the Character panel (as detailed in Step 6 of this Chapter) you are going to activate the colour/color box:

> Place cursor within the box "Color" and click (see picture III.T)

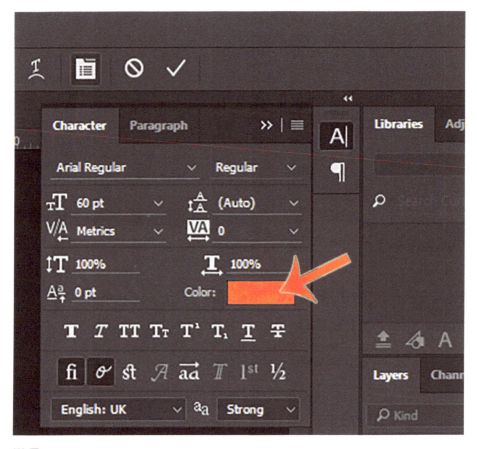

III.T

> Now move your cursor across to your image – you will see the cursor has changed its shape to that of an Eyedropper Tool icon

> Click anywhere on your image for the colour you want to use

> Click OK when happy with your colour choice (see picture III.U)

III.U

> Notice your text changes to same colour instantly

> *Memorida: Select colour for author name –*
> *Repeat the points in Step 7 of this Chapter for*
> *author's name*

> Close the Character and Paragraph panels by clicking on the four horizontal bars (see picture III.V)

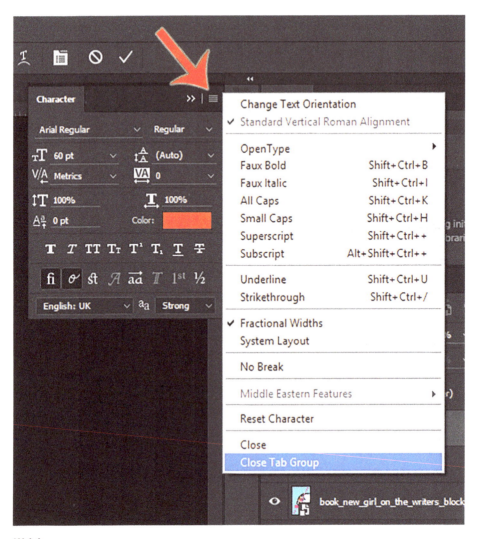

III.V

> From the drop-down menu, select Close Tab Group (highlighted
   in blue in picture III.V)

Step 8 –

Moving Text into a Different Position on your Cover:

> Click on the text layer in layers panel so it turns a lighter grey

> Press V on your keyboard

> Notice the Move Tool is highlighted at top of vertical Tool Bar (see picture III.W)

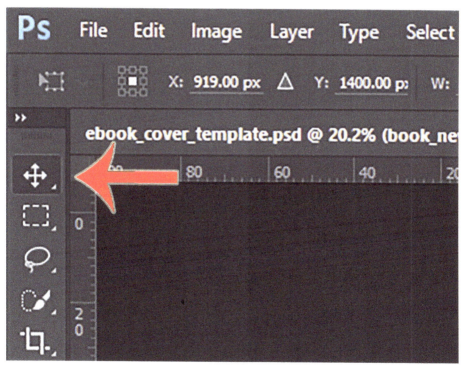

III.W

> Move your mouse around and the text moves too, alternatively

> Use the arrows on your keyboard

Memorida: Recalling the fonts you chose –
Ensure you record the font names you have picked
for your eBook cover, these will be needed when
you begin your interior book formatting

Step 9 – Remove the Yellow Margin around your eBook

> Go to layers panel

> Click on Yellow Safety Border layer (see picture III.X)

III.X

> Right click your mouse, you will see a menu appear (see III.Y)

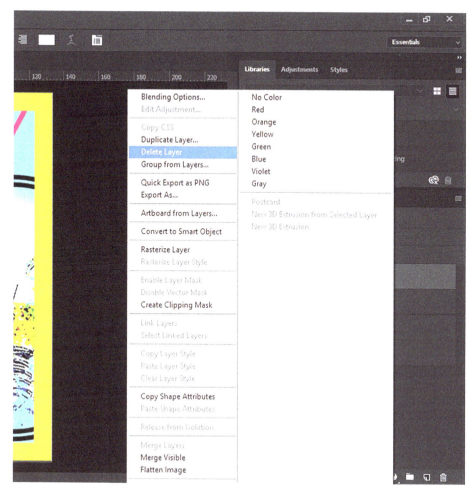

III.Y

> Select Delete Layer

> A pop-up box will come into view with the message "Delete the
  layer ...?" (see picture III.Z)

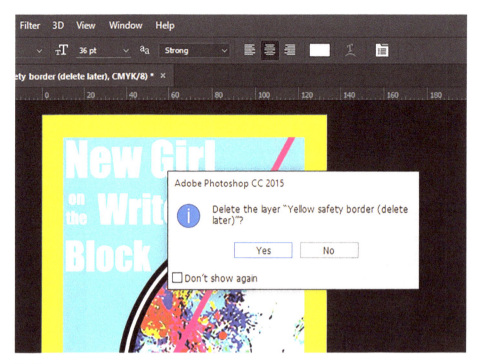

III.Z

> Click Yes

Alternatively, after picture III.X (shown earlier):

> Go to horizontal Tool Bar

> Select Layers

> Choose Delete Layer

Now delete the "White Foundation Layer" using the same method

Step 10 –

Flatten and Save your eBook Cover

Design:

> Go to Layer (in the horizontal Tool Bar)

> Flatten Image (see picture III.AA)

III.AA

IMPORTANT! – Before you save your file, check the colour mode (eBook covers need to be RGB, not CMYK), go to:

> Image in horizontal Tool Bar
> Select Mode
> Select RGB Color (see picture III.AB)

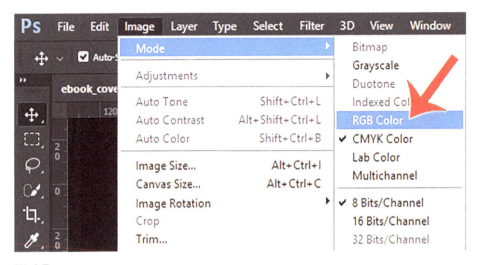

III.AB

> You may see a pop-up box stating, "You Are About To Convert To RGB ..."
> Click OK

Now go to:

> File
> Save As
> Name the file YourTitle_ebook_cover
> Save As .jpg

This is my example of an eBook cover without the yellow margins (see picture III.AC) to be saved as a .jpg

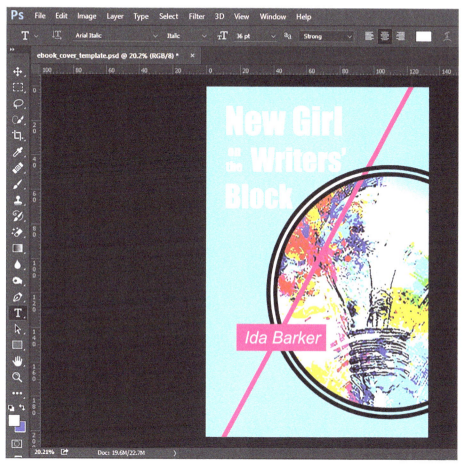

III.AC

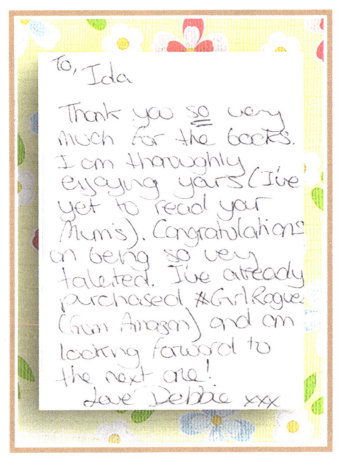

Note from Debbie at Orvis regarding #Entrangement book

Thank-you notes, especially handwritten ones, are a treat to receive

BLOG

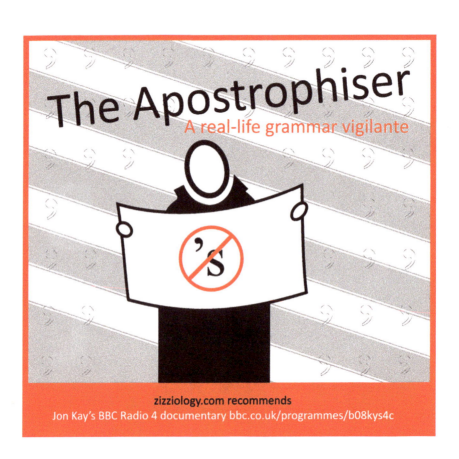

The Apostrophiser
A real-life grammar vigilante

zizziology.com recommends
Jon Kay's BBC Radio 4 documentary bbc.co.uk/programmes/b08kys4c

The Apostrophiser: a real-life grammar vigilante

Since 2013 an anonymous "grammar vigilante" has been making his mark by correcting bad punctuation displayed on Bristol's shop front signs and placards

The mysterious man, who operates in the late hours, regularly camouflages rogue apostrophes with self-engineered stickers through the use of an eight foot adapted long stick and custom-built ladder; admitting to his nocturnal activites to interviewer **Jon Kay**, **for BBC Radio 4**, he denied committing a crime, quote:

> "It's more of a crime to have the apostrophes wrong in the first place."

He went on to disclose his campaign began when a council sign displayed: Open Monday's to Friday's

Hear the documentary "**The Apostrophiser**" by **Jon Kay** at:
bbb.co.uk/programmes/b08kys4c

The 12 COMMANDMENTS of an AUTHORPRENEUR

Creativity

#3

Thou shalt NOT

design one's own book cover and moreover NOT include a picture of oneself on the front!!

Ego-go - strikes rather than strokes

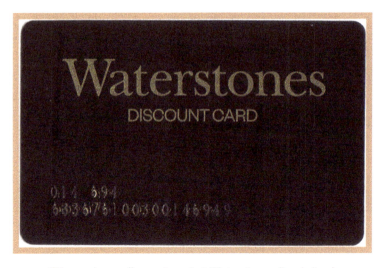

IB's employee discount card at Waterstones (bookshop)

Perks of the job included 50% discount off all books, first book I bought using this advantage was the Writers' & Artists' Yearbook - invaluable!

4

Nancy Mitford
had been lent a villa
so she could finish her book:
Oh really, what exactly
is she reading?

- Dame Edith Evans

IB (aged 15) the day after experimenting with a home hair dye kit

In the next Chapter, we return to Styles, whilst acknowledging, bad-hairstyles are thankfully, not the same thing

Format your paperback interior

Opt-in for Options

You have two options in going forward from here, either continue to work on formatting your manuscript in Word using your own .doc file or you can opt to place your manuscript into my downloadable interior template

> *Memorida: Unfamiliar to Microsoft Word? –*
> *There are many online tutorials available for free if*
> *you are seeking to familiarise yourself with Word*
> *before going forward with this Chapter*

Note-This: In the downloadable interior template I have formatted different paragraphs for a Script, Play, Musical, Novel and Poetry book (they all vary slightly to each other) – picture references of these Styles are grouped together in Step 13 of this Chapter, so you can create these Styles for yourself within your own .doc file

Step 1 –

Download the Paperback Interior Template:

> Go to GirlLikeYou.online/self-publish-your-book-templates.html

> Key in this password to gain access: GLY665463

> Save the .doc file to your chosen location

> Open the .doc file

> Click File, then

> Save As, renaming this file as your own book interior

Looking at the paperback interior template:

If you place your cursor in front of a paragraph within my template, the Style for this paragraph will be highlighted within the Styles dropdown menu (to the right of your screen) it will appear to have a blue edge surrounding it (see picture IIII.A)

Note-This: If you wish to create Paragraph Styles while working from your own Word .doc file – click on the New Style icon – located at the bottom of Styles dropdown menu, to the left (see picture IIII.A) this will open the pop-up box, from there you can programme each New Style

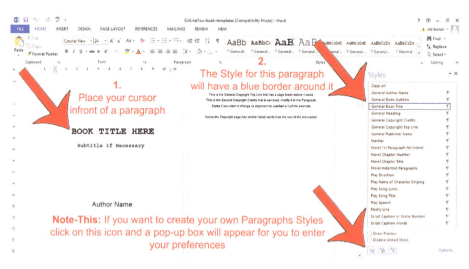

IIII.A

Page 1 of the paperback interior template is the Title page

Page 2 is the Copyright page (see picture IIII.B)

Memorida: Replacing text with your own –

All text within the template is to be replaced with your own, once you have had a quick tour of the template, the next stage will be to copy and paste your manuscript into place

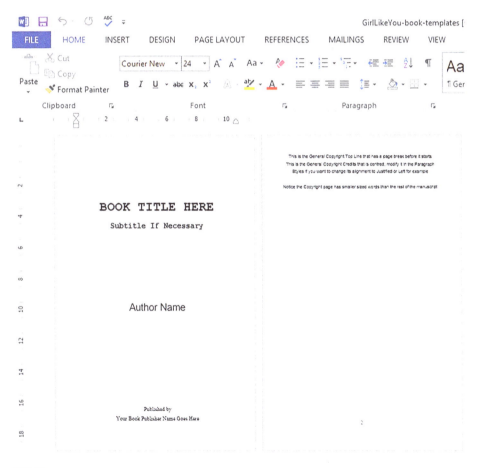

IIII.B

Page 3 of the template shows the layout for a TV/Film Script; while Page 4 has an example of song lyrics if your TV/Film Script is a Musical (see picture IIII.C)

Note-This: Later you will be able to modify the Styles to suit your own preferences – such as changing the fonts I used for Headings, to the fonts you chose to use on your eBook and paperback covers in order to give your book a more quality look

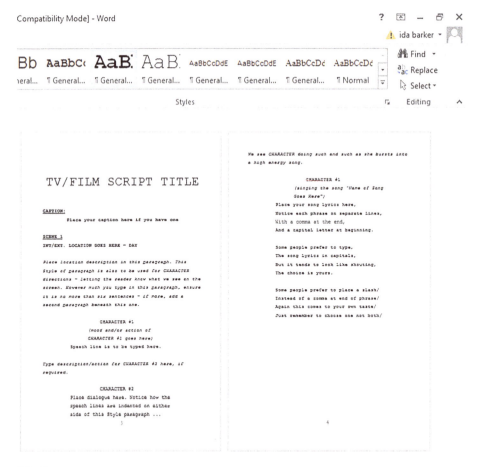

IIII.C

Pages 5 and 6 show an example of a Play layout, including song lyrics if this is a Musical Stage Play (see picture IIII.D)

IIII.D

Page 7 shows a Novel layout, notice the first paragraph in the Chapter is not indented, while all subsequent paragraphs have an indent on the first sentence only (see picture IIII.E)

Page 8 is the simplest format of all, as this is designed for Poetry. Each line of phrase within the verse is centered (see picture IIII.E)

You can see the names of all the Styles I have created in pictures IIII.F and IIII.G

1

(Novel) Chapter Title Goes Here

This is the first paragraph of a chapter, therefore, traditionally it is not indented.

Whereas all the other paragraphs that follow within this chapter will have an indent (0.76 cm) but only on the first line of each paragraph.

Feel free to alter the font and its size to your preferred look if this is not how you want your manuscript to be designed.

Notice I have formatted the Chapter Title to appear in italics – again you can change this if you wish – simply:

> Press Alt+Crtl+Shift+S to open Paragraph Styles
> Place cursor next to paragraph you want to change
> The paragraph will now be highlighted in Styles
> Hoover cursor over the Style
> Right Click
> Click Modify
> Make your changes in the pop-up box
> Click OK when you are happy!!

7

(Poetry) Verse Title

Place your line of Poetry here,
Notice each line is centred,
And is separated by a comma,
And starts with a capital letter.

You can alter the alignment so it,
Is Left rather than centred,
Or change the font and size,
By modifying the Paragraph Styles.

Whether the format you choose is a,
Script, Play, Musical, Novel or Poetry,
I hope this template serves you well,
And helps you on your beginnings,
To become a self-published author.

THE END

This template is designed by She And The Cat's Mother book publisher in connection with book, #SmileeYou, How to Format Your Script, Play, Musical, Novel or Poetry and Self-publish to eBook and paperback

8

IIII.E

IIII.F – For a continuation of this image see picture IIII.G

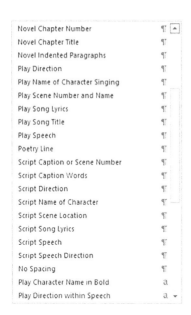

Novel Chapter Number	¶
Novel Chapter Title	¶
Novel Indented Paragraphs	¶
Play Direction	¶
Play Name of Character Singing	¶
Play Scene Number and Name	¶
Play Song Lyrics	¶
Play Song Title	¶
Play Speech	¶
Poetry Line	¶
Script Caption or Scene Number	¶
Script Caption Words	¶
Script Direction	¶
Script Name of Character	¶
Script Scene Location	¶
Script Song Lyrics	¶
Script Speech	¶
Script Speech Direction	¶
No Spacing	¶
Play Character Name in Bold	a
Play Direction within Speech	a

IIII.G

Note-This: In the Paragraph Styles I created – where it is named General, this is meant to be used across all formats: Script, Play, Musical, Novel and Poetry (see picture IIII.F)

Note-This: Look at two of the Styles (last two in picture IIII.G) to the far right of each Style is the letter a (compared to other Styles which have a paragraph icon). This highlights these two Styles are used on characters (letters) not a full paragraph of characters (letters)

Memorida: Like for like –

If copying and pasting your manuscript into the interior template ==> to change each of your paragraphs to a pre-programmed Style, just place your cursor in front of each paragraph, then click on a Paragraph Style listed in the dropdown menu

Step 2 –

Transfer your Manuscript to the Paperback Interior Template:

> Open your paperback interior template

> Open your manuscript

> Copy your complete manuscript

> Paste your complete manuscript into your template

Memorida: Your paperback's dimensions –
The downloadable paperback interior template's trim size is 5.25 inches x 8 inches (13.3 cm x 22 cm or 132 mm x 202 mm) the dimensions of most trade paperbacks – all print-on-demand (POD) companies offer this size in white and cream paper. However, it's easy to change the size of your paperback, just follow Step 3 of this Chapter

Step 3 –

Select the Trim Size for your Interior Paperback .doc:

> Go to Page Layout

> Go to Page Setup

> Go to Paper

> Go to Height and Width and enter your preferred size

> Here you can also alter the margins

Memorida: No-no, to mean-girl margins –
You will notice I have mirrored the pages, the outer
edges should always be more generous than
those of industry standard to prevent your text
being too near the book's spine

Step 4 –

Arrange your Front Segments (example below):

Note-This: Separate each segment with a Page Break: (for this procedure see Step 7 of this Chapter)

> Page 1: Book's Title and Author's Name

> Page 2: Copyrights; permissions; ISBN (barcode number)

> Page 3: Start of Manuscript

Step 5 –

You May Want Other Pages – such as:

> Praise or a foreword

> Dedication

> About the Author

> Other books by Same Author

Once you have explored the Paragraph Styles within this Chapter you will be able to format such features yourself

Step 6 –

Apply Custom Styling Where You Don't Want Normal

You will now apply custom Styles to areas where you do not want Normal, such as your headings, first paragraphs of new chapters without indents, front and/or back matter:

> Place cursor at beginning of text that you want to change

> Drag cursor/mouse to highlight the region

> Press Alt + Ctrl + Shift + S (or go to Home tab; click Styles arrow)

> A selection of Styles to choose from will appear

> Choose one of the Styles, or to create your own Style, just:

> Click New Style (button lower left corner of Styles screen)

> Rename and define the Style you want

> Change fields of font and size to your preference

> Do not click OK yet; see Step 7 following

Step 7 –

Separate Segments i.e. Chapter Headings with a Page Break

Whilst in Create New Style From Formatting box:

> Go to Format tab

> Click Paragraph

> Click on Line And Page Breaks on box ribbon

> Tick Page Break Before box

> Click OK

Memorida: The copyright page –

Ensure you choose smaller text for the copyright page compared to that in the rest of your book

Step 8 –

If a Style you Created is Not How you Like, then Modify:

> Place cursor at beginning of text you want to change

> Drag cursor/mouse to highlight the region

> Press Alt + Ctrl + Shift + S (or Home tab and click Styles arrow)

> A selection of Styles to choose from will appear

> Hover cursor over the Style you want to alter

> Click on the arrow next to the Style, or right click your mouse

> You will see a drop down menu

> Select Modify

> Change the fields to your preference

> When you are ready click OK

Step 9 –

Apply Character Styling to Italics, Bold and Underline

Do not forget to apply "character" instead of "paragraph" in Style Type when Styling your words

> Place cursor at beginning of word/sentence you want to change

> Drag cursor/mouse to highlight the region

> Press Alt + Ctrl + Shift + S (or go to Home tab; click Styles arrow)

> A selection of Styles to choose from will appear

> Choose one of the Styles, or

> To create your own character Style, just:

> Click New Style (button lower left corner of Styles screen)

> Rename

> In Style Type

> Select Character (NOT Paragraph)

> Change fields to your preference i.e. Click on Bold

> Click OK

Note-This: You may not have realised but in Styles theme box – Automatic is the colour black

Memorida: Caution inserting italics, bold and underlined –
Ensure only the word or sentence is italicised, not the spaces, full stops and/or paragraph marks before and after the italicised area. This applies to bold and underlined characters also

Step 10 –

For Good Practice do not Indent the First Line of a Chapter for a Novel

To remove an indent from the first line of a chapter:

> Highlight the paragraph you want to affect

> If working in downloaded interior template:

> Open Styles

> Select Novel 1st Paragraph No Indent

> Or, Create a No Indent paragraph yourself in New Styles

> Rename and define the Style you want, by going to:

> Format

> Paragraph

> Indents And Spacing

> Special

> Select None

> Click OK

Note-This: To separate paragraphs in nonfiction use a line space, but not for fiction

Step 11 –

When Formatting Headings in Styles:

> Heading should be centered

> Heading should be larger in size to the main body of text

> Heading should have a font that is the same as your Book's title

Step 12 –

If you are Using Images:

> Place cursor where you want an image to go in your manuscript

> Go to Insert tab, then to Illustrations

> Click Picture

> Choose your picture

> Click Insert

> Right click on inserted picture

> Select Format Picture (or Size, or Size and Position)

> Click Size tab (if you've selected Format Picture)

> Tick boxes beside Lock Aspect Ratio, and

> Boxes Relative To Original Picture Size

> Modify percentage next to Height or Width to your preference

Memorida: Prepare your pictures –

Ensure your images were saved in a PDF print-ready format; at least 300 DPI, scaled to size, and in either RGB (for CreateSpace and all eBooks) or CMYK (for IngramSpark) mode

Note-This: In Chapter 6: Go Sign Up with a Distributor, I outline the differences between companies CreateSpace and IngramSpark

Step 13 –

Ida's pre-programmed Paragraph Styles

If working from your own Word .doc file rather than downloading my paperback interior template, you could create New Styles of paragraphs (button lower left corner of Styles screen) yet type the same entries as mine within the pop-up boxes for your manuscript:

13A: General – Headings and copyright page

13B: Script for TV/Film (plus TV/Film Musical)

13C: Play for Stage (plus Stage Musical)

13D: Novel

13E: Poetry

13A: GENERAL STYLES

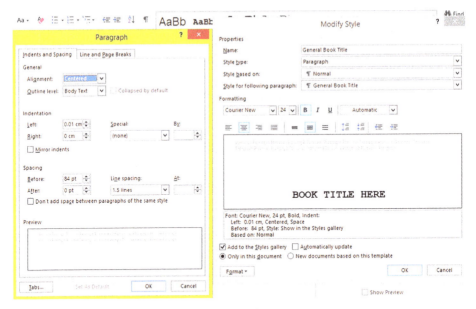

IIII.H – Title Page (Book Title Name)

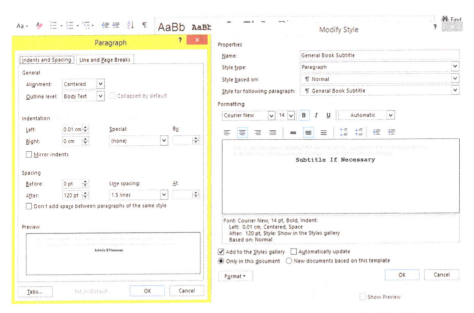

IIII.I – Title Page (Subtitle) – If you do not have a subtitle, then you

should alter "Book Title Name" Style (see picture IIII.H) Go to:

Indents and Spacing; Spacing; and in After enter 120 pt. rather than leaving it at 0 pt.

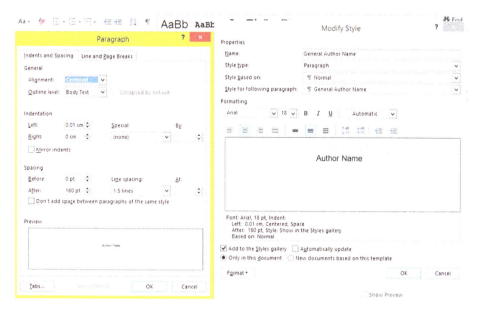

IIII.J – Title Page (Author Name)

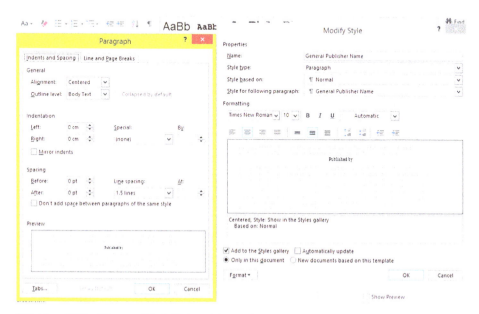

IIII.K – Title Page (Published by ...)

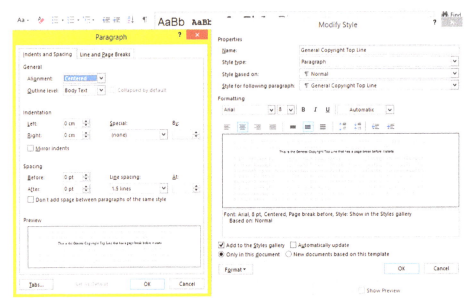

IIII.L – Copyright Page (Top Line)

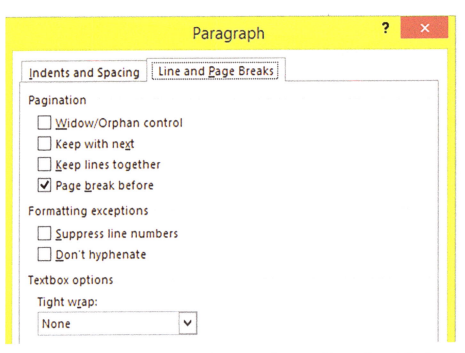

IIII.M – Copyright Page (Top Line must have a Page Break before)

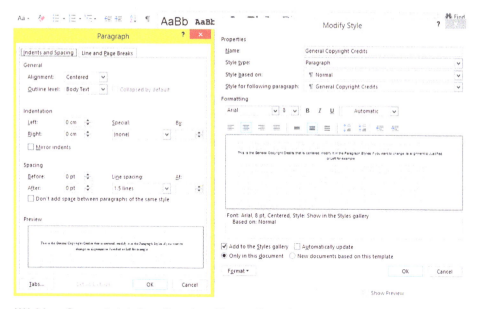

IIII.N – Copyright Credits (no Page Break, ensure box is unticked)

13.B TV/FILM SCRIPT STYLES

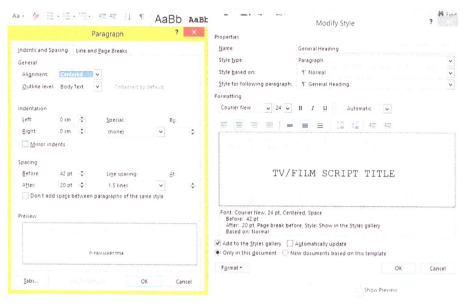

IIII.O – Script Heading (ensure a Heading has a Page Break before; like that of picture IIII.M shown earlier in this Chapter)

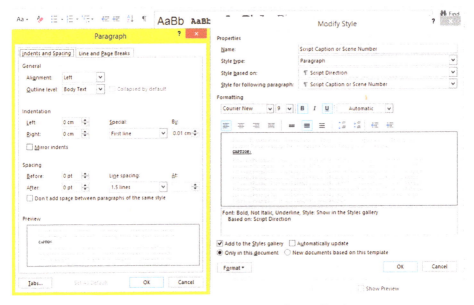

IIII.P – Caption or Scene Number Style for a Script

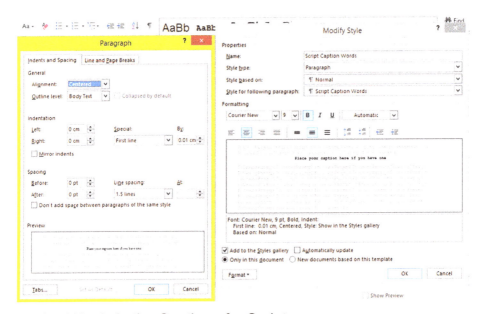

IIII.Q – Words in the Caption of a Script

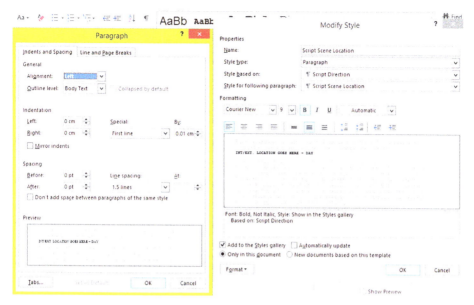

IIII.R – Scene Location Style of a Script

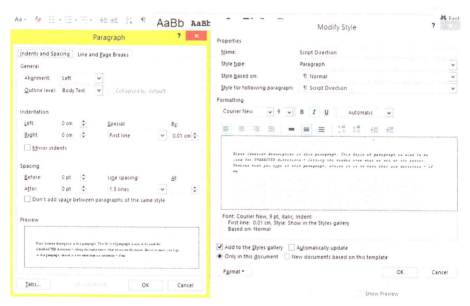

IIII.S – Description/Action within a Scene Style of a Script

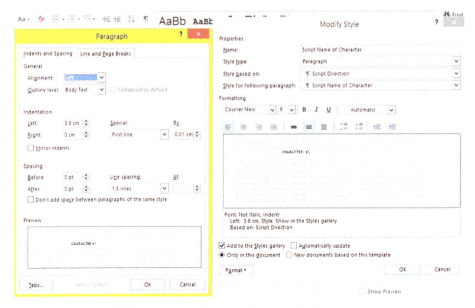

IIII.T – Name of Character Style within a Script

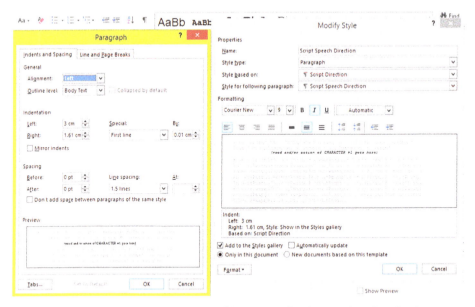

IIII.U – Direction placed within Character's Speech of a Script

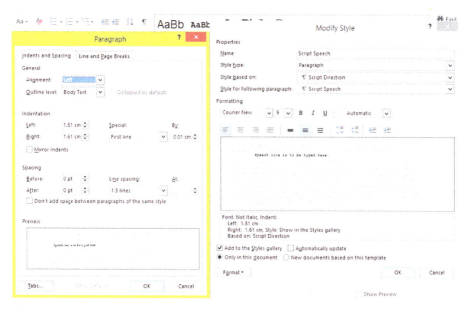

IIII.V – Speech Paragraph Style within a Script

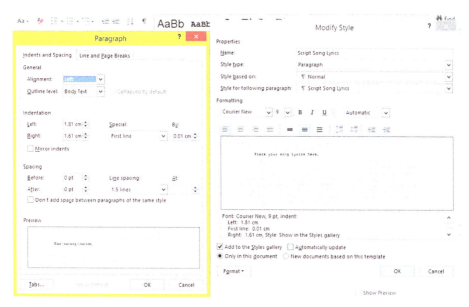

IIII.W – Paragraph Style for Song Lyrics within a TV/Film Musical Script

13C: PLAY STYLES

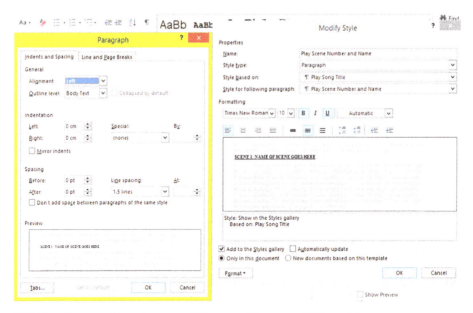

IIII.X – Scene Number and Scene Name within a Play

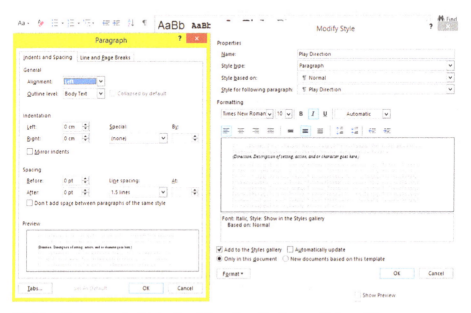

IIII.Y – Paragraph Style for Direction/Action within a Play

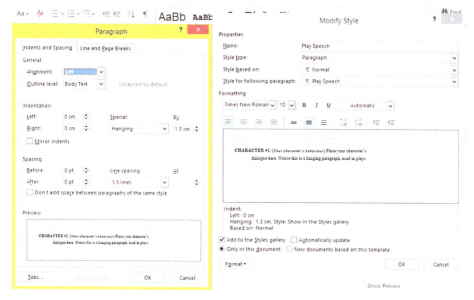

IIII.Z – Paragraph Style for Speech within a Play

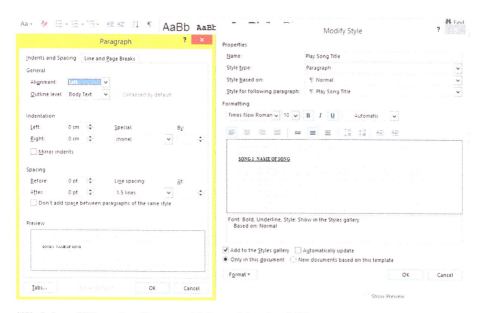

IIII.AA – Title of a Song within a Musical Play

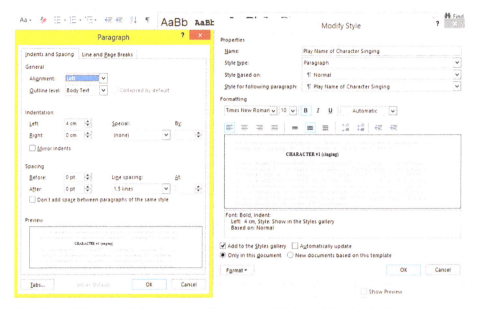

IIII.AB – Name of Character Singing within a Musical Play

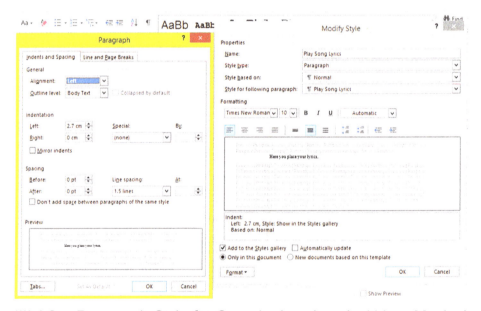

IIII.AC – Paragraph Style for Song Lyrics placed within a Musical Play

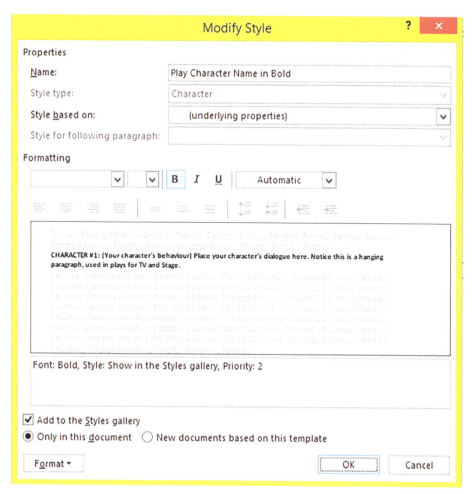

IIII.AD – This is not a Paragraph Style, but a Character Style: Notice in the Preview window of this picture, the name of the character at the start of the paragraph has a bold format ...

To use this Style, simply highlight with your cursor, your character's name within the paragraph and select this Style from the dropdown menu or Create New Style yourself

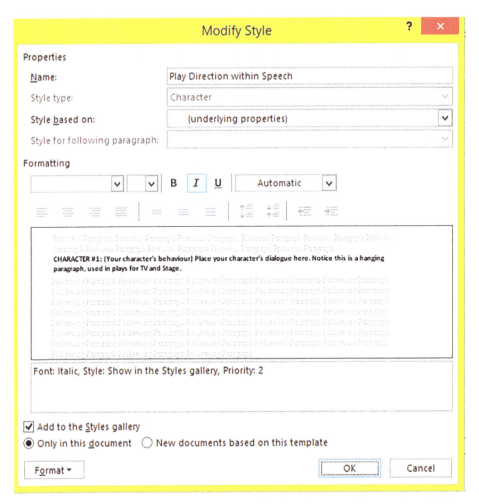

IIII.AE – This is not a Paragraph Style, but a Character Style: Notice in the Preview window of this picture, the direction in brackets has an italic format ...

To use this Style, simply highlight with your cursor, a selection of words within a paragraph that you want to have this effect and choose this Style from the dropdown menu or Create New Style yourself

13D: NOVEL STYLES

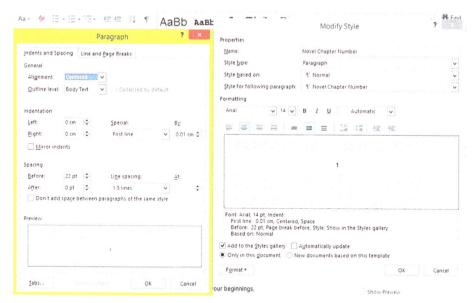

IIII.AF – Chapter Number within a Novel (ensure this Paragraph Style has a Page Break before; ref picture IIII.M for an example)

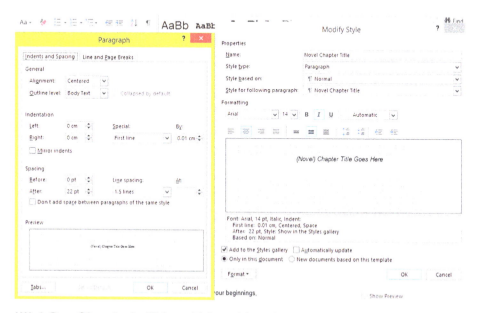

IIII.AG – Chapter's Title within a Novel

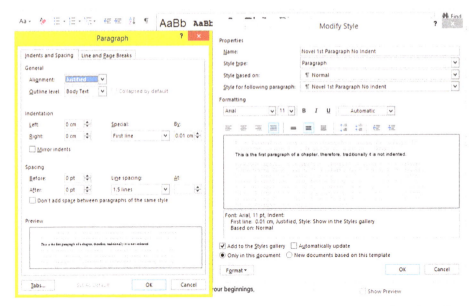

IIII.AH – This Novel Paragraph Style is to be used for the first paragraph of a new chapter only, as it has no indent

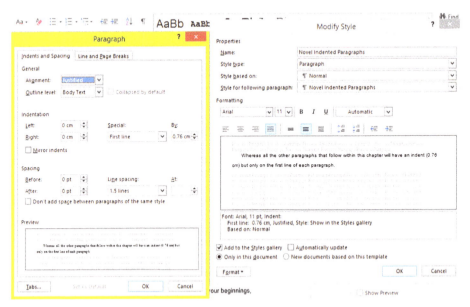

IIII.AI – This Novel Paragraph Style is to be used for paragraphs what follow the first – it has a first line indent of 0.76 cm

13E: POETRY STYLES

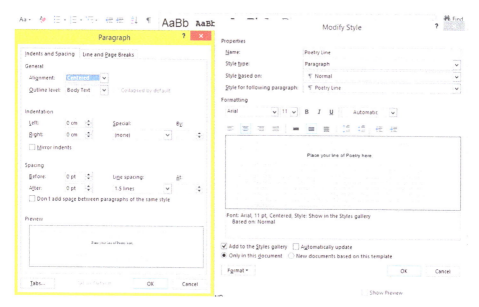

IIII.AJ – Each Poetry line/phrase in your verses should use a separate paragraph, and either have an alignment that is centered or to the left – I have chosen centered, but by all means tweak the Style to your preferred look!!

Step 14 –

Remember to Embed Fonts:

> Open your interior paperback

> Go to File

> Word Options

> Select Save

> Choose Embed Fonts

> Click OK (see picture IIII.AK)

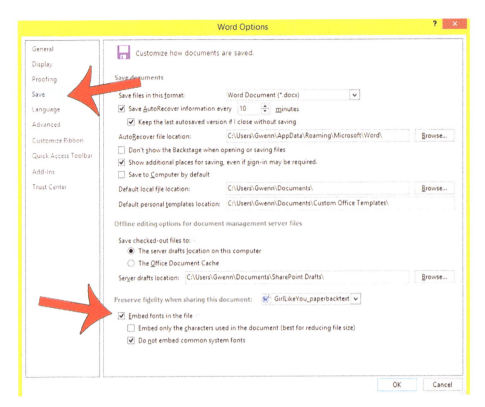

IIII.AK

> Close document

Memorida: I have unsightly page numbers everywhere?! –

You may have noticed page numbers inserted onto every page. Do not fret #GirlLikeYou. Any page numbers you do not require will be removed manually later

BLOG

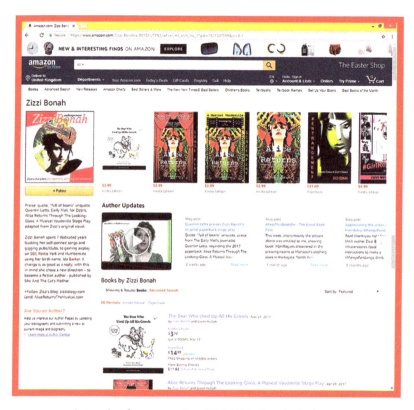

Screenshot from computer of ZB's US Author Central page

Are you promoting yourself on Amazon Author Central?

A place where Amazon authors and their readers connect ...

If you are a US / UK author of any book listed within Amazon's catalogue you are eligible to sign up by logging on - (using your existing Amazon account) - to their Author Central network via:

authorcentral.amazon.com and authorcentral.amazon.co.uk

Amazon guides you through the set up process - and following account confirmation, the benefits include:

==> Adding your books to your bibliography
==> Submitting your author biography
==> Posting author pictures - (most recent always shows first)
==> You can even add video

US account enables you to add your RSS feed - (to display your blogs)

The 12 COMMANDMENTS of an AUTHORPRENEUR

Originality

#4

Thou shalt NOT

produce the SAME story as everyone else

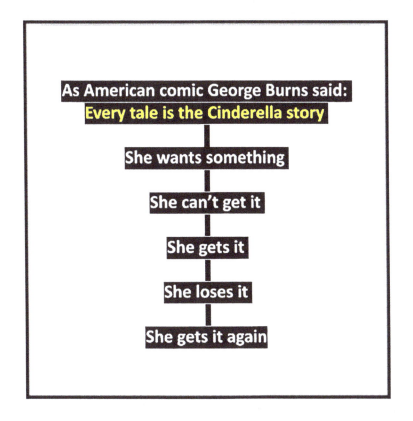

As American comic George Burns said:
Every tale is the Cinderella story

She wants something

She can't get it

She gets it

She loses it

She gets it again

Why break a winning formula?

Passionfruit cocktail: picture taken by IB at The Den, Harrogate

*It takes plenty of passion
to become a self-publisher*

5

My mistakes are as much responsible
for making me who I am
as my achievements

- Hilary Devey CBE
entrepreneur

"

29/7/93

● SHOWING off their design are (clockwise from top) Ida Barker, Eve Skinner, David Stowe, Ashley Ward, Tahera Kahnum and sculptor Sahaja Maher.

Creative scrap is modern art

CREATIVE pupils at Bridlington School spent a week transforming scrap metal into modern art with the help of Leeds sculptor Sahaja Maher. Sahaja, who divides his time between sculpting and Buddhism, was working on the theme of 'Magic and Transformation'. Sahaja and the Year 9 pupils set about 'transforming scrap into something magical'.

Article within local newspaper

When opportunity knocks

Not one of the students (pictured above) had set eyes on this artwork before we were cajoled into posing alongside it, nevertheless, we acted accordingly

Save your paperback interior to a press-ready file

Shortcuts do not Pay, no Matter How much they Cost

For this segment you will be embracing Adobe Acrobat Pro – do not be tempted #GirlLikeYou to use Adobe Reader, it does not have all the features you shall need to move forward successfully with this chapter

Step 1 – Converting your Paperback Interior .doc to .pdf:

> Open Adobe Acrobat Pro

> Click on File

> Select Open

> Choose "All Files" in box that opens up (see picture V.A)

V.A

> Select your edited interior paperback .doc

> It will take a moment to convert to a PDF, then

> Save As, YourTitle_for_printing in your desired place

Note-This: You can save your document as an Adobe PDF from Save As if you have a newer version of Word

Step 2 –

Remove any Page Numbers you do NOT Require

For example: those on pages at the beginning of your book before Chapter 1; those just displaying an image; and/or blank pages:

> Open your YourTitle_for_printing PDF

> Go to Tools (see picture V.B)

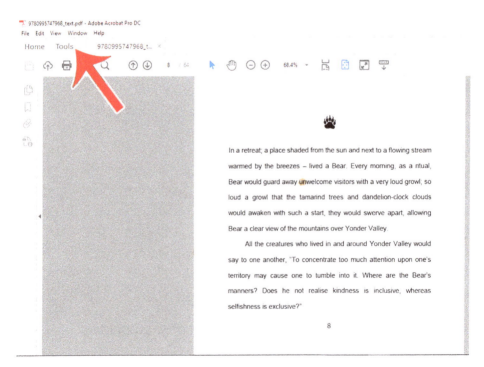

V.B – example manuscript: The Bear Who Used Up All His Growls

> Select: Edit PDF or Advanced Editing or Edit in some versions (see picture V.C)

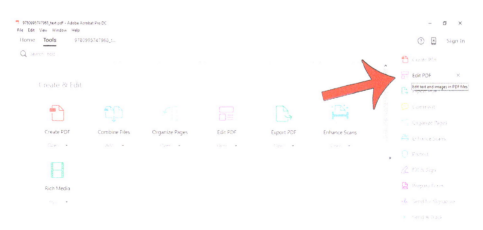

V.C

> Place cursor behind each page number you do not want, or highlight the page number with your cursor (see picture V.D)

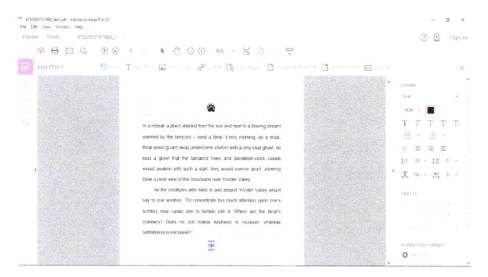

V.D

> Press Delete key

Step 3 –

How to Save your File:

> Go to File

> Save As Other

> Press-Ready PDF (see picture V.E)

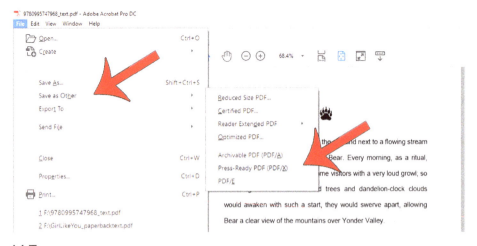

V.E

> Name your file: YourISBN_text

> In Save As Type: select PDF/X (*.pdf)

> Click on Settings (see picture V.F)

V.F

> A Preflight pop-up box will be actioned

> Tick box for setting PDF/X-1a (see picture V.G)

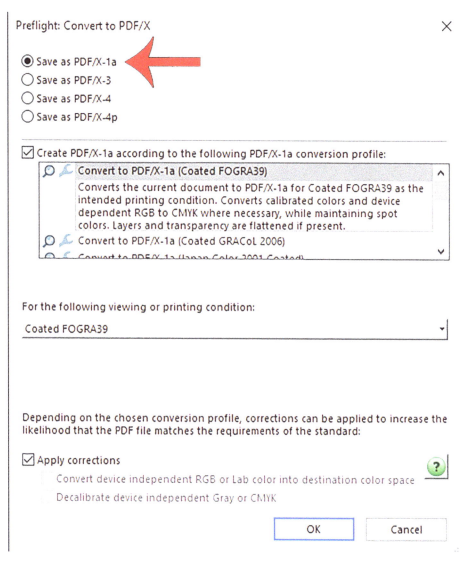

V.G

> Click OK

Calling cards

front and back

Designed by She And The Cat's Mother; printed by vistaprint

ZB's first business cards

B
L
O
G

You'll Notice Me, cos I'm Not Dressed as a Playing Card

Zizzi Bonah

You'll Notice Me, cos I'm Not Dressed as a Playing Card,
is a short story within book, #GirlRogues: Braggadocio

How do you dress for duress in times of hardship?

Hedda Hopper was known for wearing flamboyant hats to draw singular attention to herself. A visual identity, a sartorial signature to affirm her celebrity. But more importantly - self-preservation

People who are notable for a particular manner of dress are protected in hard times, because their signature outfit represents a lifetime

A signature outfit says all by itself: Here is who I am, no matter what's going on right now - any momentary bad spell will disappear - it helps remove the person from reality, **like a character in a film or a book**, so long as they are reasonably successful - then - is the presumption of success about them

The 12 COMMANDMENTS of an AUTHORPRENEUR

Photoshopping

#5

Thou shalt NOT

create photoshopped banners of celebrities to rise one's profile

You have to be on your Metal and go for it

Finding new story ideas

Sometimes the unobtainable becomes obtainable

When Chris Evans returned with TFI Friday in 2015 on C4 - he said a certain pop star - known for no longer smiling - did so because she'd "used up all her smiles" -

from Chris's imaginative words I began penning a fantasy story - now included in #GirlRogues: Braggadocio

zizziology.com

155

Bouquet: picture taken by IB at Chelsea Flower Show, London

Flowers of fine thoughts
from me to you

6

I must not trail behind
as the Lapwing trails her wings

- Lady Claudette Wrothwaite, fictional character from short story:
Home Front, within book Silver Splitters: Tales of the Unsuspected
by GH

Waterwheel: picture taken by IB at Chelsea Flower Show 2013, London

*Keep the wheel turning to gain the reward
and turn to the next Chapter*

Go sign up with a distributor

Nothing is Achieved without Action

Example: When I needed to know how to insert my Alice Returns Through The Looking-Glass musical audiobook into my WordPress website, I Googled "insert audio files to WordPress" the search led me to the answer: add /wp-admin to the end of my www. address

And in a Similar Way, you Must Action yourself into the Next Stage

Action: sign up to a print-on-demand (POD) distributor – whereby you inform them of your paperback's dimensions, page count and page colour – this information enables the distributor to create a paperback cover template for you, (containing the all important spine width) only then can you design an accurate paperback cover for yourself

Through experience I champion two distributors:

Option 1 – CreateSpace

CreateSpace.com is owned by Amazon. As it is registered in America, you will have to enter your (TIN) tax identification number. If you are not living in the United States this will mean applying for one via the US government (usually takes 6 weeks). Alternatively, if you have already registered in your home country for filling out a tax return (i.e. as an individual sole trader or partnership), you will be assigned a tax number – this can be used in place of a TIN

Advantages –

Using CreateSpace means you can self-publish without spending any money. They will issue your paperback with an ISBN (a barcode) free of charge!

Disadvantages –

The downside to CreateSpace is your printed book will only be available on Amazon, unless you pay a fee

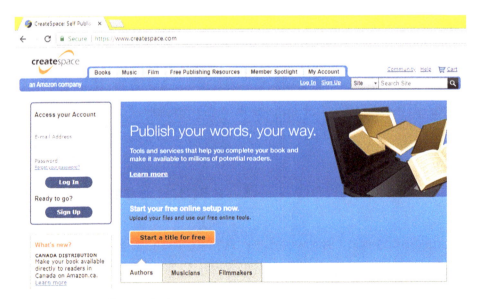

VI.A – CreateSpace's home page

Regarding ePublishing – Kindle Direct (kdp.amazon.com) means your eBooks will be exclusively available for Amazon Kindle

Option 2 – IngramSpark

IngramSpark.com is the sister company to Lightning Source

You will pay a small fee for each paperback/eBook you release

Advantages –
Using IngramSpark gives you access to a long list of retailers they distribute to. And, encouragingly, it is both a print and ePub distributor – making your eBooks available for iBooks, Apple and Kindle

Disadvantages –
You will be required to purchase your own ISBNs (barcodes) from your country, however this can be an advantage as you are credited as the publisher to retailers, compared to CreateSpace, whereby they are labelled as the publisher due to the fact they supply the ISBN (barcode)

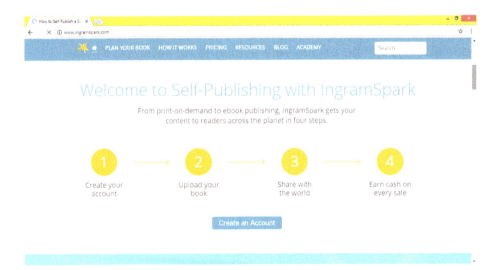

VI.B – IngramSpark's home page

Put your #GirlLikeYou Google Goggles on and Research

I encourage you to read up on both options to see which you prefer regarding your time, money, and the percentage of royalties that will be shared between you and the distributor

Where to Purchase ISBNs (barcodes):

Australia: myidentifiers.com.au

Great Britain: isbn.nielsenbook.co.uk

Canada: bac-lac.gc.ca

United States: isbn.org

Note-This: If your country is not listed in this Chapter, you can search the directory of ISBN agencies and find your respective national ISBN registration agency at: isbn-international.org

Memorida: Be barcode savvy –

You cannot assign the same ISBN (barcode) to your paperback and eBook – even though they are the same book, they are recognised as different products, and must therefore have individual ISBNs

IB's hot chocolate drink topped with cream and smarties

Before you ask, no this is not part of my "keep healthy regime" #TreatYourself

BLOG

Fantasy Fiction book title generator

designed by zizziology.com

1st letter of your first name		1st letter of your surname		1st letter of your county/state	
A	Beautiful	A	Outlaw	A	Devoted
B	Last	B	Phoenix	B	Light
C	Strange	C	Face	C	Hour
D	Heaven's	D	Descent	D	Calling
E	Uneasy	E	Creatures	E	Return
F	Mystery	F	Son	F	Gates
G	Rightful	G	Mistress	G	Mirror
H	Golden	H	Storm	H	Gain
I	Hidden	I	Rider	I	Wind
J	Company	J	Feast	J	Vain
K	Rebel	K	Prince	K	Phaze
L	Iced	L	Saga	L	Moon
M	Banished	M	Gift	M	Dreamer
N	Stolen	N	Raven	N	Dance
O	Tomorrow's	O	Empire	O	Throne
P	Chosen	P	Lords	P	Constitute
Q	Nameless	Q	Cares	Q	Blue
R	Marcid	R	Soul	R	Enduring
S	Mine	S	Dioptric	S	Stars
T	Forgotten	T	Pillars	T	Far
U	Overnight	U	Queen	U	Hill
V	Fair	V	Unicorn	V	Underworld
W	Alphabet	W	Fever	W	Shadow
X	First	X	Song	X	Blade
Y	Waiting	Y	Steward	Y	Wild
Z	Northern	Z	Code	Z	Fallen

of the

Example: Zizzi Bonah from Yorkshire:
Z = Northern, B = Phoenix, Y = Wild
Northern Phoenix of the Wild

Using the book title generator above, here are a few of my family and friends would-be book titles:

Rightful Storm of the Wild
Forgotten Creatures of the Stars
Uneasy Gift of the Moon

Write your title here: ....

Your family and friends: ....

....

....

Generating book title ideas

It's all in a name

I don't know about you, but I won't press pen to paper, or fingers to keyboard unless I have a **working title** in place. And when ideas are running clear cold, sometimes we all need a kick-start from a voice outside ourselves

Look no further

Whether you've finished writing your manuscript or merely interested to know what your **family and friends** book titles could be within the fantasy fiction genre - here is a book title generator I've designed after discovering a fabulous blog by **Tara Sparling** - (tarasparlingwrites.com) - **Tara**'s book title generators include Chick-Lit, Literary, Crime, and Auto-biography - (but not fantasy!!)

View fantasy fiction book title generator

on the page opposite ...

dictionary
definition of word:
GENERATE, vt.
(generating, generated).
To beget; to produce;
to cause to be

The
12 COMMANDMENTS
of an
AUTHORPRENEUR

Excess

#6

Thou shalt NOT

use long book titles - less is more

#ENTRANGEMENT
Where Colours Don't Bleed

"He saved her life, only she can save his death"

Salt Delray, wrongfully imprisoned for the murder of her lover, Rhuand Mezarron - the unrivalled Kielter of the Metalgants: ruled by Female Munrah. But Rhuand is not dead! He roams the Gardenia Lake in limbo - betwixt the cycle of elements and the infinite above. Salt is vital to his salvation.

Mission:
Salt must escape and enter a hidden underworld to reunite with Rhuand, and together, battledore against Female Munrah and her subordinates; which soon turns into a very different and terrifying reality.

Your Invite!

Become a BonBon Heart by following Zizzi Bonah's blog site at:
zizziology.com

*Ten syllables including hashtag -
if you say it quicker, it sounds shorter*

The above image is taken from a section of the book's back cover

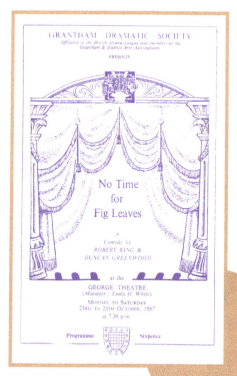

GRANTHAM DRAMATIC SOCIETY
(Affiliated to the British Drama League and members of the Grantham & District Arts Association)

PRESENTS

No Time for Fig Leaves

A Comedy by
ROBERT KING &
DUNCAN GREENWOOD

at the

GEORGE THEATRE
(Manager Louis H. White)

MONDAY TO SATURDAY
23RD TO 28TH OCTOBER, 1967
at 7.30 p.m

Programme   Sixpence

GB (nee Hullah)

CAST
(In order of appearance)

MONICA SHARPE (P.P.S. to Constance Claythorne)	GWEN BARKER
CONSTANCE CLAYTHORNE (Prime Minister)	SUSAN RICKARD
DORA	ELAINE BULPETT
LYDIA PARKER (Minister of Science)	JAN BOLAM
W.COMDR. NIGEL LAWLER, R.A.F.	BRIAN PROCTOR
MAJOR DANVERS BISHOP	RUBY GOODALE
PROFESSOR DAVID MOXTON	DAVID BOLAM
HELEN MARCHBANKS, W.R.N.S. (First Lord of the Admiralty)	HILDA DEWEY
CPL. EVE FOSTER, W.R.A.C.	JILL CRAGG

PRODUCED BY
ARTHUR HARVEY

No Time For Fig Leaves production 1967

Day-job: window-dresser at Chambers (fashion) of Grantham

7

Some folk believe less is more, from where I come from more is more and less is less

- Lesley Garrett CBE

soprano

Tour De France sculpture: pictures by IB at Montpellier Hill, Harrogate 2017

If you look for inspiration, you will find it

This "Alice-like" door carved into a 100 year old Elm tree, inspired a chapter within ZB's book: Alice Returns Through The Looking-Glass

Request your paperback cover template

Put in your Request

Following your decision to sign up with a print-on-demand (POD) company – either CreateSpace or IngramSpark – the next stage is to request your paperback cover template for download

Option 1 – CreateSpace:

> Search: CreateSpace.com/Help/Book/Artwork.do

> A box will appear (bottom left), Configure Your Template

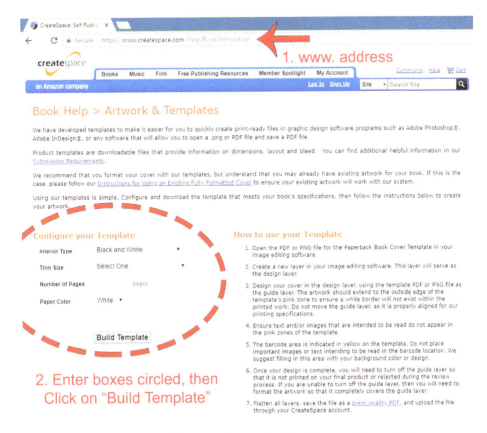

> After filling in your paperback's details, Click Build Template (see picture VII.A)

> In a moment your template will be ready for download

> Click where it states, Click Here To Begin Download (see picture VII.B)

> Save the download file to your chosen place

Memorida: What to use and what not to use –

All content will be in a zip folder: there you will see both a PNG and a PDF file; you will only be using the PDF

VII.B – Screenshot of CreateSpace's ready for download template

Option 2 – IngramSpark:

> Log in to IngramSpark

Enter into a new browser tab the following:
https://myaccount.ingramspark.com/Tools/
CoverTemplateGenerator, then

> Fill in your paperback's details (see picture VII.C) it is not mandatory to enter your book's retail price – so leave this blank
> Enter your email address, then
> Click Submit
> Within moments you can start checking your emails for the cover template (attached), once received
> Download PDF template to your chosen place

Memorida: Barcode image and barcode number – IngramSpark will place an actual barcode (image: black and white stripes, along with a number code above and below the stripes) onto your paperback cover template, therefore you are not required to purchase a barcode image from another company to place within your design. Whereas, CreateSpace will place an actual barcode onto your paperback after you have uploaded your design

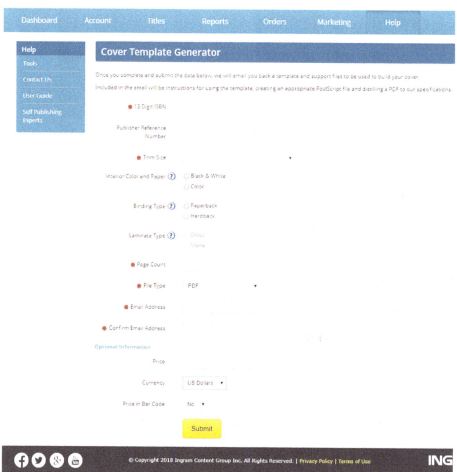

Cover Template Generator

Once you complete and submit the data below, we will email you back a template and support files to be used to build your cover.

Included in the email will be instructions for using the template, creating an appropriate PostScript file and distilling a PDF to our specifications.

* 13 Digit ISBN

Publisher Reference Number

* Trim Size

Interior Color and Paper (?)   Black & White   Color

Binding Type (?)   Paperback   Hardback

Laminate Type (?)   Gloss   Matte

* Page Count

* File Type   PDF

* Email Address

* Confirm Email Address

Optional Information

Price

Currency   US Dollars

Price in Bar Code   No

Submit

VII.C

BLOG

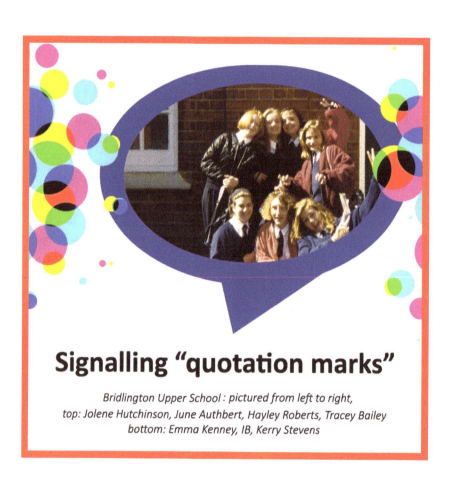

Signalling "quotation marks"

Bridlington Upper School : pictured from left to right,
top: Jolene Hutchinson, June Authbert, Hayley Roberts, Tracey Bailey
bottom: Emma Kenney, IB, Kerry Stevens

BLOG

Misspellings in TV subtitles can lead to story ideas

In September 2015, Ross King was interviewed on ITV1's popular day-time programme: This Morning, about his second book of fiction: Breaking Hollywood. His first book being: Taking Hollywood. He joked his third would be called Baking Hollywood - Killed by a Croissant. However, the TV subtitles spelt out: Killed by a Question

This misspelling inspired a chapter within my forthcoming book. Have you turned a blunder into a writing opportunity?

And when some people should come with subtitles
Whilst taking driving lessons, part of the directions a driving instructor gave his student were as follows, (as told to IB by Nicola Isherwood):

Instructor: Make a left turn here
Student: Okay
Instructor: Now, I want you to take note of the cycle path
Student: (pause) The psychopath ...?
Instructor: No. The cycle path!

Ref: subtitles provide a transcript of the television soundtrack, helping deaf and hard-of-hearing viewers, (or those who don't want their tv volume loud) to follow programmes

The
12 COMMANDMENTS
of an
AUTHORPRENEUR

Endorsements

#7

Thou shalt NOT

use celebrity endorsements
to elevate one's products,
the quality of your work
should speak for itself

"beautifully published"

Dame Julie Walters' praise

for **Gwen Hullah's paperback**

Safe In Killer Hands: The Original Screenplay

Julie Walters

Dear Gwen + 9da,

beautifully published

Julie Walters

This paperback is available from Amazon; published by She And The Cat's Mother

Too good not to share

The above banner was posted on author, GH's social media sites

Coffee beans: picture by IB at Chelsea Flower Show 2013, London

Jumping beans, there's plenty in this picture to replemish anyone's energy levels!! Coffee time ...?

8

Rather like politics, continuity is vital

– Stella Asquith, fictional character in novel:
Safe In Killer Hands: Money, Madness, Murder
by GH

Title: The Chavie
Artist: Gwen Barker (nee Hullah)

As a self-taught artist from line-drawing to impressionism, I posted this photograph of my watercolour painting: **The Chavie**, to **Piers Morgan**, then, the **Editor of The Mirror** newspaper: with a proposal to use this image for their charity event

Piers personally replied, kindly stating, regretfully, an image had been selected and printed. He did not return the photograph of my painting

I treasure his lovely letter, the size of a label on a jar of homemade pickle, which is in such a safe place that for the life of me, I cannot find it ... GH

194

Create your paperback cover

Creation Station

Energy does not disappear, it just moves to another place – with this in mind, successfully you downloaded your paperback cover template, now you can start creating your paperback cover look. A note to mention here: the examples in this Chapter refer to IngramSpark's template, while it is not dissimilar to CreateSpace, be assured any differences will be highlighted when and where they arise

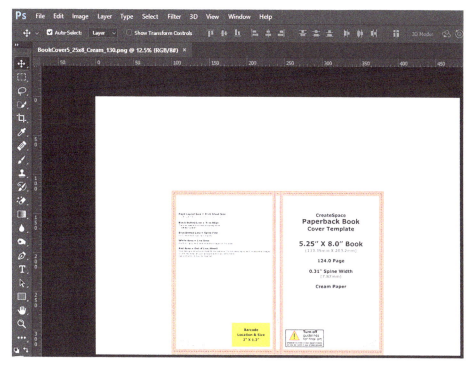

VIII.A: This is what a CreateSpace template looks like – compared to IngramSpark's shown throughout this Chapter

Step 1 –

Open your Paperback Cover Template in Photoshop:

> Open Adobe Photoshop, then go to File

> Locate and open your paperback template

> Ensure boxes are filled in as picture VIII.B, click OK

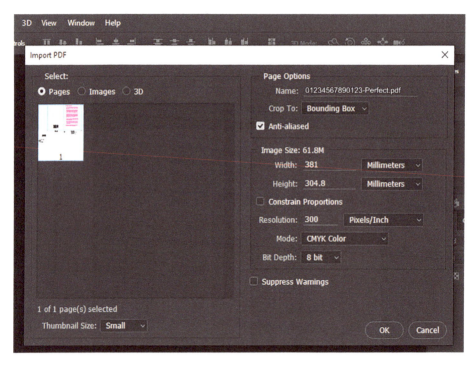

VIII.B

Note-This: Differences – Colour Mode:

> Type CMYK Colour in IngramSpark's Mode box

> For CreateSpace: when you open its template, automatically it

will have the colour mode of RGB: view picture VIII.A again – above ruler is the file name, next to which is the colour mode: BookCover5_25x8Cream_130.png @ 12.5% (RGB/8#)

Recap: IngramSpark's paperback colour mode must be CMYK. CreateSpace's paperback colour mode (and all images for eBook including cover) must be RGB

Step 2 –

Save As YourISBN-perfect.pdf and

choose your Preferred Destination

Your IngramSpark template will look similar to picture VIII.C

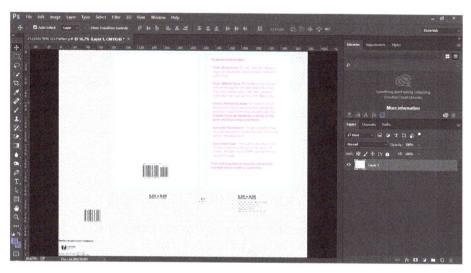

VIII.C

Step 3 –

Delete areas on your template (by using the Eraser) to create transparent areas

IngramSpark ONLY:

You are going to delete all pink areas on the template, creating transparent windows for your design, while allowing the blue guide lines to remain as the top layer

CreateSpace ONLY:

You are going to delete everything within the red guide lines on the template – all text and white areas – BUT NOT THE YELLOW RECTANGLE, creating transparent windows for your design, while allowing the red guide lines to remain as the top layer

Note-This: Referencing picture VIII.A – you will see a yellow rectangle on CreateSpace's template – this is where the barcode will go. Do not delete this. Unfortunately, you cannot move the barcode to a different area on the cover as CreateSpace state its location must remain in place

Memorida: Transparent areas? – Grey and white
checks on the template show transparent areas

> Press E on your keyboard to activate Eraser Tool – notice the Eraser is highlighted in the vertical Tool Bar, see picture VIII.D

VIII.D

Ensure you choose a large eraser as selected in picture VIII.E

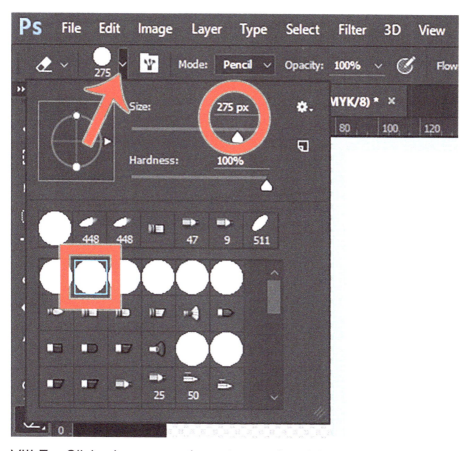

VIII.E – Click where arrow is, enter number (circled) tool (squared)

> Move your cursor across to the template

> Left click (and hold) while moving your cursor across the screen
   and over the pink text in IngramSpark's template (black text for
   CreateSpace)

> Instantly you will see the Eraser Tool working by revealing a
   transparent area (see picture VIII.F)

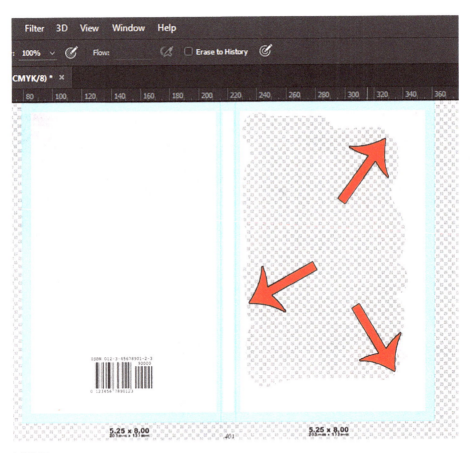

VIII.F

You shall return to deleting the rest of the pink areas on
IngramSpark's template, once you have duplicated the barcode

Step 4a – Differences
Barcode – ONLY for IngramSpark
Template!!

You must duplicate your barcode into another layer, here's how:

> Press M on your keyboard to initiate Rectangular Marquee Tool

> Drag cursor around the barcode image

> A dotted line now surrounds barcode (see picture VIII.G)

VIII.G

> Copy and paste by pressing Ctrl + C and then Ctrl + V

> You will notice a new layer has been added in the layers panel

> Rename that layer Barcode, by:

> Double-clicking the text of the layer

> Immediately it can be renamed (see picture VIII.H)

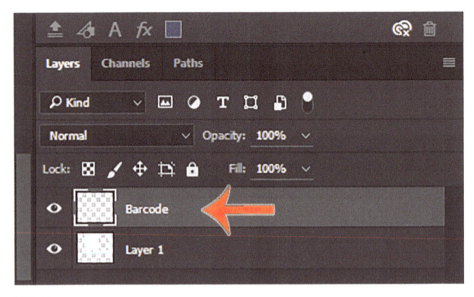

VIII.H

Note-This: Move this barcode layer anywhere on your back cover

Step 4b – Differences

Barcode – ONLY for CreateSpace

Template!!

CreateSpace will insert a barcode onto your paperback cover after you have uploaded your design, therefore the procedure mentioned in Step 4a for IngramSpark is not needed here

Step 5 –
Continue with Eraser Tool to create transparent areas on template

Ensure Layer 1 is highlighted in the layers panel, then:

ONLY for IngramSpark template, move your Eraser across the barcode in the original layer to delete it (see picture VIII.I)

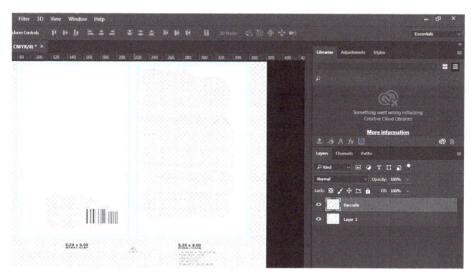

VIII.I – Barcode in Layer 1 is deleted

Now, for both IngramSpark and CreateSpace templates, move your cursor across to the Eraser Tool in the vertical Tool Bar, then:

> Right click

> Three Eraser icons will appear, you must

> Click on the icon with three stars – this is known as the Magic
  Eraser (see picture VIII.J)

VIII.J

> Move your cursor back to the template

> Click on the remaining areas of pink (or white for CreateSpace)
  within your coloured guide lines, and

> As if by magic, the colour you want to delete will vanish!!

You should now be left with a tidy template, (see picture VIII.K)
showing plenty of transparency, ready for the next stage – inserting
your eBook cover onto your paperback cover template

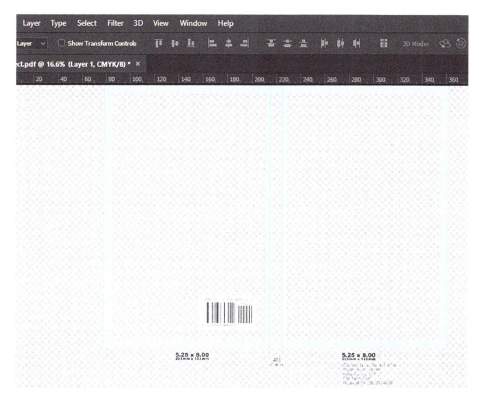

VIII.K

Step 6 –

Insert your eBook Cover onto Paperback Cover Template:

> Go to File

> Select Place Embedded or Place

> View pop up box requesting a file

> Find the .jpg file you created of your eBook cover

> Click Place

Note-This: Even though the eBook cover was saved as a .jpg with the colour mode of RGB, IngramSpark's template will convert it to colour mode: CMYK once the .jpg is placed within the template

> Move your eBook design onto the right side of template, by
> Using your keyboard arrows
> Ensure cover's text is within guide lines, if image falls short this will be corrected later (as with picture VIII.L)
> Click the tick in the horizontal Tool Bar to place the image (see picture VIII.L – tick circled in red)

VIII.L – image falls short at top of template

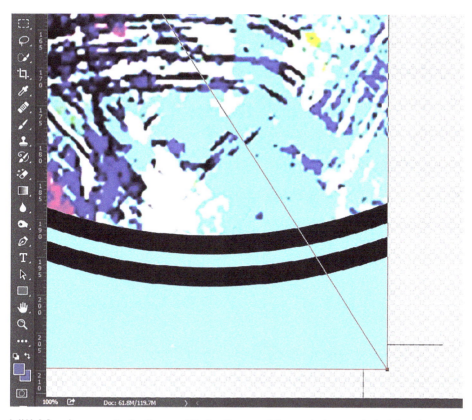

VIII.M – image is in line with bottom of template and right edge

VIII.N – eBook cover placed on template with Layer 1 at front of other layers, so easy to see what part of image is in safe zone

209

Step 7 –

Options when Designing left side/back of Paperback Cover Template:

==> insert a block of colour

==> insert a mirror image of the front cover (or)

==> insert a different image

To Insert a Block of Colour:

> Activate Rectangle Tool by pressing U on computer

> Place cursor top left and draw a rectangle over back cover area

> Double-click your new layer in Layers Panel, (renamed it Back Block or similar)

> Choose a complimentary colour to your front cover (method described in Chapter 3: Step 7)

To Insert a Mirror Image:

> Repeat Step 6 of this Chapter using a text-free image

> Go to Edit

> Transform

> Flip Horizontal (see picture VIII.O)

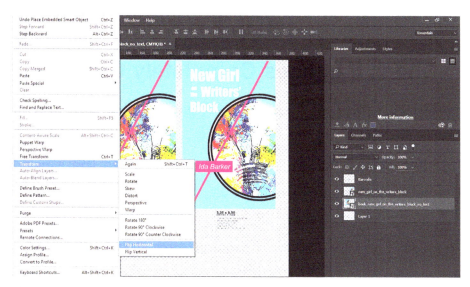

VIII.O

A mirror image should look similar to picture VIII.P – notice the spine is still image free for the moment

VIII.P

To Insert a Different Image:

Repeat Step 6 of this Chapter – but place a different image file from your computer

Step 8 –

Check if Images Completely Conceal

Trim Areas of Template

It is bad practice to see the light blue line (or red line if using CreateSpace) around the edge of your book cover

Remedy: put into practice the same method you used when copying the barcode – only this time choose a Narrow Piece of the image next to the area of concern, then:

> Rename this new layer

> Go to Edit

> Transform

> Flip Horizontal (or Vertical if going from left to right)

> Move the Narrow Piece into place

In my example I used this procedure for both the top edges of the paperback and also the spine (see picture VIII.Q)

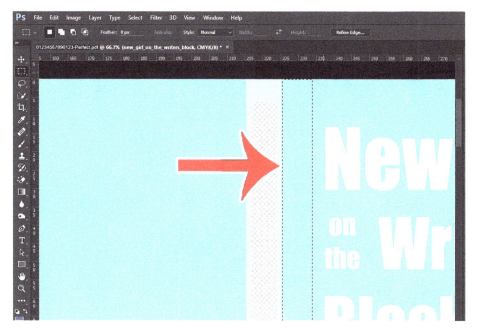

VIII.Q – copying a section of the image from top to bottom in order to cover the full length and width of the spine

Step 9 –

Combine Images into One by Using the Merge Layers:

> Click eBook cover layer within layers panel so it highlights

> Hold down the Ctrl button, and

> Click Narrow Piece(s) and Back Cover layer

> View all layers highlighted (see picture VIII.R)

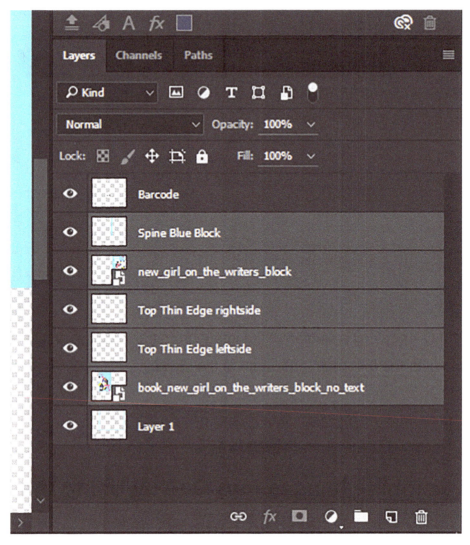

Layers Channels Paths

Kind

Normal   Opacity: 100%

Lock: Fill: 100%

👁 Barcode

👁 Spine Blue Block

👁 new_girl_on_the_writers_block

👁 Top Thin Edge rightside

👁 Top Thin Edge leftside

👁 book_new_girl_on_the_writers_block_no_text

👁 Layer 1

VIII.R

Then,

> Over one of the selected layers, just

> Hold cursor

> Right click, and

> Choose Merge Layers (see picture VIII.S)

> Rename this merged layer to Paperback Cover Image

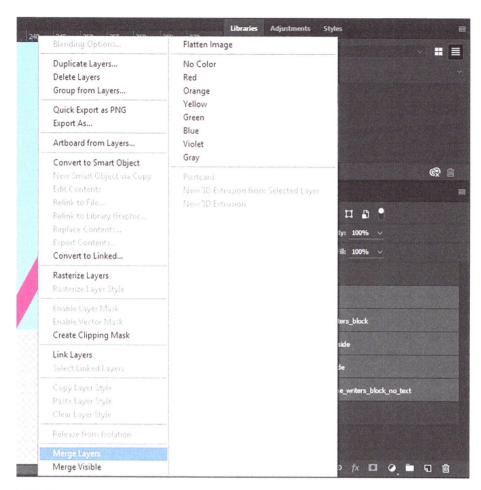

VIII.S

Step 10 –

Erase Cover Edges that Overlap onto Transparent Areas (this Step is NOT Necessary if Using CreateSpace):

> In the layers panel choose Cover Image layer

> Activate Eraser Tool by pressing E on keyboard

> Select Soft Round 100 Pixels brush

> Hold down the Shift key, and

> Slowly drag cursor along each edge of your cover

Note-This: Do not be too eraser enthused – take care to only erase parts of the image that exceed the outer guide lines

Step 11 –

Place Text onto your Back Cover:

> Press T

> Place cursor and click on area where you want text to appear

> Start typing your text, or

> Copy and paste your prepared text into where the cursor flashes

> Adjust font style, size, colour and alignment to your preferred look, (see picture VIII.T) by:

> Using the horizontal Tool Bar

> If needed, use mouse or arrows to reposition text

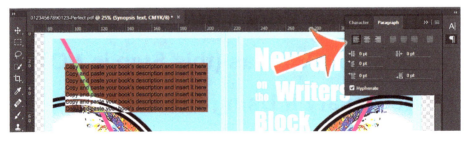

VIII.T

Step 12 –

Place Text onto your Spine:

> Use general text method as mentioned earlier, then

Rotate text by going to:

> Edit

> Transform

> Rotate 90 degrees Clockwise (see picture VIII.U)

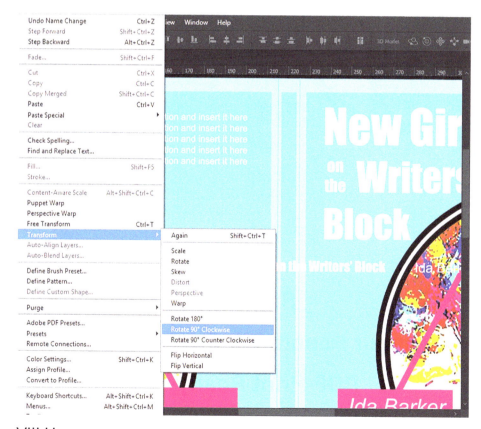

VIII.U

> Position the text into place between the inner guide lines (see picture VIII.V)

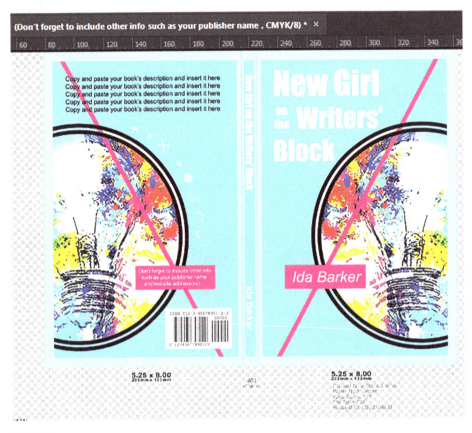

VIII.V

Step 13 –

Save your Paperback Cover Design to a PDF Print Ready File

Ensure you save a copy of your design as a .psd file first, go to Save As and use the name YourISBN_cover, then:

> Go to Layer

> Flatten Image (see picture VIII.W)

VIII.W – flattened image of the paperback cover (notice all transparent areas have disappeared)

Then, go to:

> File

> Save As

> Rename your file as YourISBN_cover

> Choose Photoshop PDF (see picture VIII.X)

> Click Save

> If a box pops up informing you settings will be overridden:

> Click OK (see picture VIII.Y)

> You will be presented with a Save Adobe PDF box

> Select PDF/1a:2001 (in Preset and Standard options)

> Leave all boxes unticked (see picture VIII.Z)

> Click Save PDF

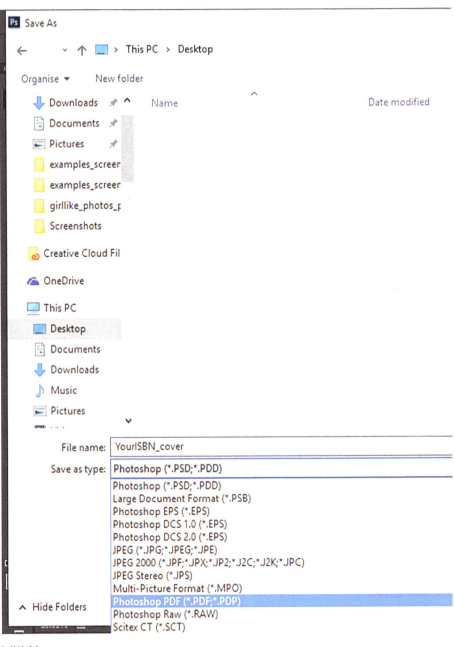

VIII.X

220

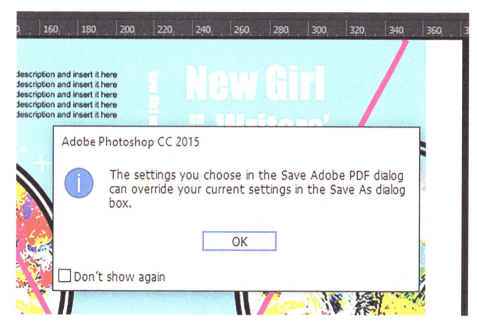

VIII.Y

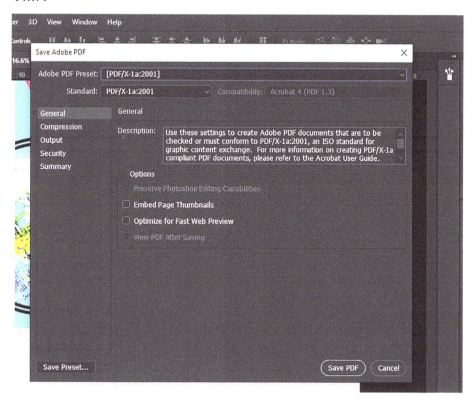

VIII.Z

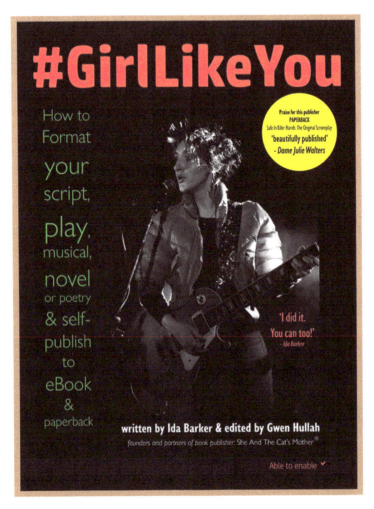

This is the alternative book cover design for the book you are reading now

*I always design two different book covers
for each book, later, we select between
the two the better one to go to print*

B
L
O
G

Which "Miss" might you be?

Miss Chief
Miss Appropriate
Miss Behave
Miss Spell
Miss Fired
Miss Demeanour
Miss Cellany
Miss Hap
Miss Guided
Miss Chance
Miss Understood
Miss This That and the Other

or perhaps one not mentioned on the list above, if so, write it below

Miss ....

The trouble with Miss Demeanour, Miss Understood and Miss Guided

Here are 3 examples ...

The perfect driver?

Miss Demeanour arrived by taxi at her destination. The irate taxi driver turned to her and said: "There'll be no charge, lady. You did most of the driving."

The perfect writer?

Miss Understood sent a number of articles to a celebrated newspaper columnist, asking his advice as to the best channel for marketing her writings. The response came back: "The one channel I can recommend as the greatest outlet for articles of this type is the English channel."

The perfect secretary?

Miss Guided - a doctor's secretary - was perplexed by an entry in the doctor's notes on an emergency case: "Shot in the lumbar region." After a moment she brightened up and, in the interest of plainness, typed into the record: "Shot in the woods."

The
12 COMMANDMENTS
of an
AUTHORPRENEUR

Popularity

#8

Thou shalt NOT

show how well-liked you are
by your friends or work
colleagues, in an attempt to
gain more book sales

Ida (AKA author Zizzi Bonah) received handwritten note from her work colleague, Katie Fraser who leaves barista-ing at Waterstones (books) Harrogate, to go to Durham University ...

Ida, (The Jam House)

I'm going to miss our Mango Fandango sessions and your wonderfully weird outbursts that always made me laugh!

Can't wait to be back in the café with you at Xmas - may the mango fandango live forever!!

we are united forever through this ¼ Indian a weird way)

Lots of love,
Katie xxxxx

How to make a mango fandango cooler

> fill glass with ice cubes & add 1/4 of cold water
> add 2 pumps of lemon & lime syrup
> top to rim with mango puree
> empty contents into blender
> blend for 8 seconds then serve

zizziology.com

A kind word goes a long way ...?

IB calling from a British Telephone box in Silema

If you want to phone a friend and let them know you need some quiet time to read this next Chapter, now's the time

9

Rules are important, but they're temporary and they're always supposed to be changed

- John Lydon
singer/songwriter

Torquay 1995: picture taken by IB

*Self-publishing is like a horse-drawn cart,
everything must pull in the same direction*

Format your eBook interior using an HTML editor

Editing the Editor

The advantage of using a HTML editor to format your eBook is it will guarantee an error-free eBook file that you can upload to any distributor and/or retailer. The process is split into two segments:

A – You will make small but necessary changes (adding codes) to your manuscript in Microsoft Word so it will transfer to HTML

B – You will download the eBook template and make it your own by copying and pasting your manuscript into it

.SEGMENT A:

Step 1 –

Open your Paperback Text in Word .doc

> Make a copy of this file and rename it: YourTitle_ebook_text

Step 2 –

Find and Format all italicised Words:

> Click Ctrl + H

> Place your cursor in the Find What section

> Click More (see picture IX.A)

IX.A

> Click Format at the bottom of the box

> Select Font from the drop down menu (see picture IX.B)

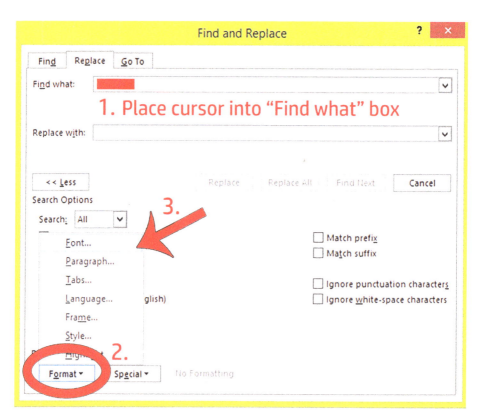

IX.B

> You will see another box pop up:

> In Font Style, select Italic (see picture IX.C)

> Click OK

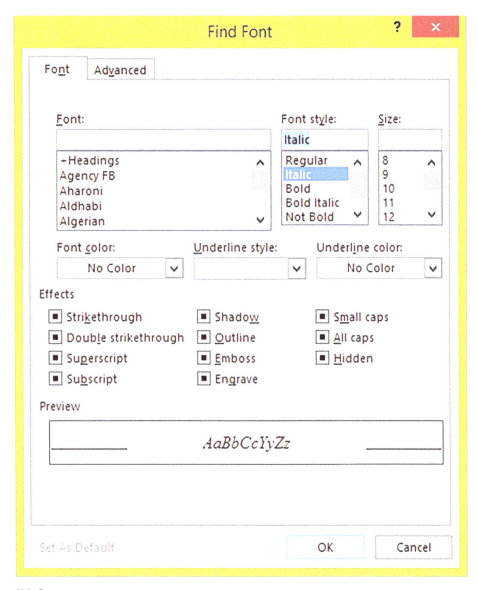

IX.C

> Insert <i>^&</i> in Replace section (see picture IX.D)

> Click Replace All

IX.D

Note-This: Every word in your Word .doc that appeared in italics will now look like this: <i>italic words</i>

Step 3 –

Find and Format Words in Bold:

Repeat Step 2 of this Chapter, but this time for bold text – instead of using <i>^&</i> use ^& (see picture IX.E)

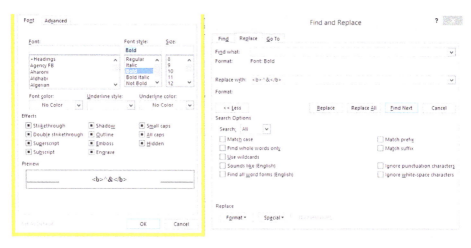

IX.E

Step 4 –

Find and Format all En-dashes (-) and

Em-dashes (–):

> Click Ctrl + H to open Find and Replace box

> Place en-dash (-) into Find What

> Type – (en-dash) into Replace

> Press Replace All (see picture IX.F)

> Also into Find What:

> Repeat the method above for any em-dashes (–) you might have

> Ensure you type — (em-dash) into Replace

> Press Replace All (see picture IX.G)

IX.F

IX.G

Step 5 – Find and Replace Accented Letters and Symbols with Code:

ACCENTED LETTER: é

CODE: é

SYMBOL: £

CODE: £

SYMBOL: #
CODE: #

SYMBOL: %
CODE: %

SYMBOL: (
CODE: (

SYMBOL:)
CODE:)

SYMBOL: *
CODE: *

SYMBOL: @
CODE: @

SYMBOL: _
CODE: _

SYMBOL: -
CODE: –

SYMBOL: –
CODE: —

SYMBOL: '
CODE: ‘

SYMBOL: '
CODE: ’

SYMBOL: "
CODE: “

SYMBOL: "
CODE: ”

SYMBOL: ...
CODE: …

FRACTION: 1/2
CODE: &franc12;

FRACTION: 1/4
CODE: &franc14;

I have listed the most common accented letters and punctuation symbols in this Step (5) using the same method as Step 4 – if you are interested to learn more possibilities, just Google "HTML punctuation symbols"

Step 6 – Format any Images Placed in your Manuscript into HTML Code:

Memorida: Colour mode –

Ensure each image has been saved as a .jpg file and has the colour mode RGB, not CMYK

> Remove each image (one at a time) from your manuscript, then

> In its place insert: <img src="YourFileName.jpg"/>

Note-This: Replace YourFileName in the above example with the actual name of your image file

And, if you would like to centre your image, use this code instead:
<img src="YourFileName.jpg"/>

Step 7 –

Download the eBook Interior Template to Begin Modifying it to your Requirements:

> Go to GirlLikeYou.online/self-publish-your-book-templates.html

> Download the eBook interior template html of your choice (password: GLY665463) choosing from:

> Script; (see picture IX.H)

> Play; (see picture IX.K)

> Novel (see picture IX.N), or

> Poetry (see picture IX.P)

> Open the template in the HTML editing programme Notepad++

> Save As, using the file name of your eBook

Memorida: What does all this coding mean? –
If you do not understand the coding at the top of
the template, do not be discouraged, I have
inserted it to save you time. If you would like to
learn more about it, go to Google

Step 8 –

Inclusion of Images:

If you are including images within your eBook, ensure you place all images, and the template you are working from, into the same folder!!

Step 9 –

How to View the HTML file in your Browser:

> Double click on the HTML file in its folder to open it

> In your internet browser – you can see what the format looks like

> By changing the size of the browser to that of an eReader you will create a similar look to the real one – (though any page breaks, such as those inserted before a new chapter, will not appear in browser)

View browser pictures: IX.I, IX.J, IX.L, IX.M, IX.O, IX.Q

IX.H – TV/Film Script (Musical) HTML Template

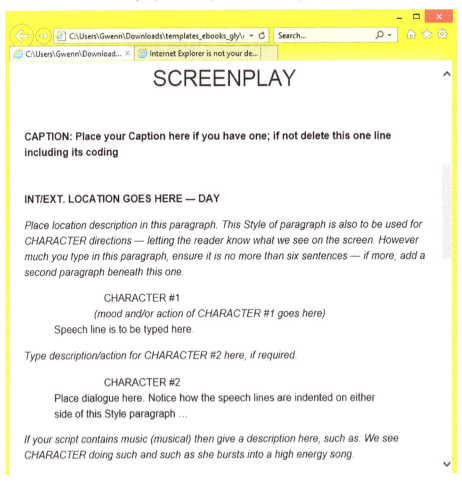

IX.I – TV/Film Script (Musical) HTML file viewed in your browser

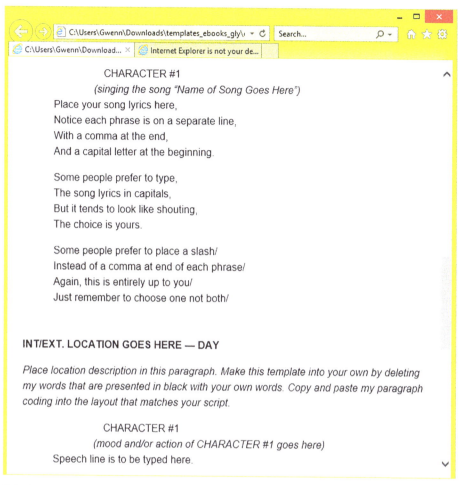

CHARACTER #1
(singing the song "Name of Song Goes Here")
Place your song lyrics here,
Notice each phrase is on a separate line,
With a comma at the end,
And a capital letter at the beginning.

Some people prefer to type,
The song lyrics in capitals,
But it tends to look like shouting,
The choice is yours.

Some people prefer to place a slash/
Instead of a comma at end of each phrase/
Again, this is entirely up to you/
Just remember to choose one not both/

INT/EXT. LOCATION GOES HERE — DAY

Place location description in this paragraph. Make this template into your own by deleting my words that are presented in black with your own words. Copy and paste my paragraph coding into the layout that matches your script.

CHARACTER #1
(mood and/or action of CHARACTER #1 goes here)
Speech line is to be typed here.

IX.J – TV/Film Script (Musical) HTML file viewed in your browser

Note-This: If your Script or Play is NOT a Musical, then remove the lines that I have placed for lyrics of a song

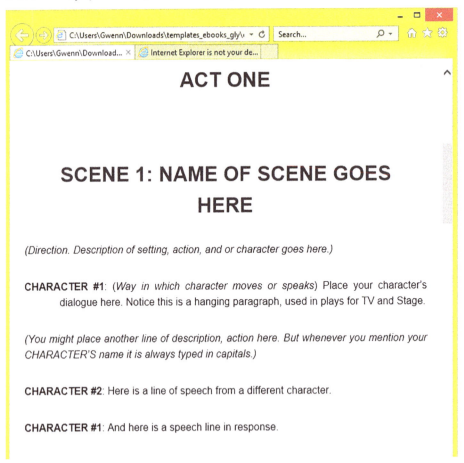

IX.K – Play (Musical) HTML Template

IX.L – Play (Musical) HTML file viewed in your browser

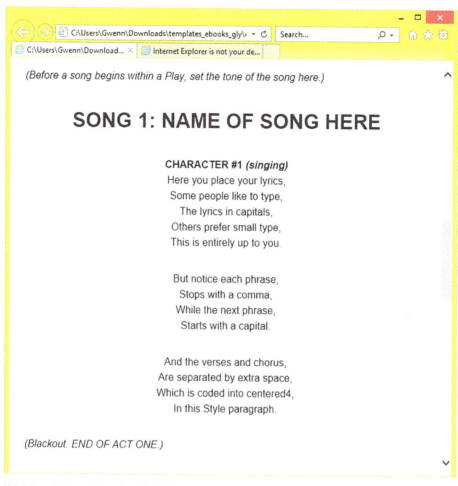

(Before a song begins within a Play, set the tone of the song here.)

SONG 1: NAME OF SONG HERE

CHARACTER #1 *(singing)*
Here you place your lyrics,
Some people like to type,
The lyrics in capitals,
Others prefer small type,
This is entirely up to you.

But notice each phrase,
Stops with a comma,
While the next phrase,
Starts with a capital.

And the verses and chorus,
Are separated by extra space,
Which is coded into centered4,
In this Style paragraph.

(Blackout. END OF ACT ONE.)

IX.M – Play (Musical) HTML file viewed in your browser

IX.N – Novel HTML Template

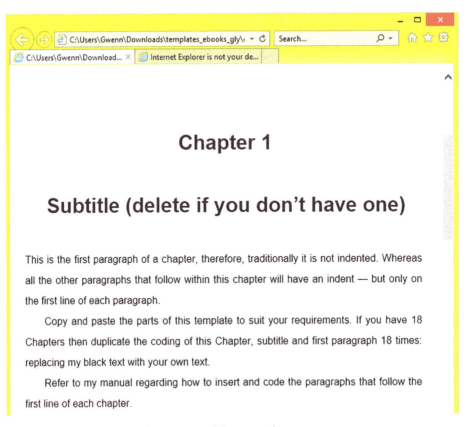

IX.O – Novel HTML file viewed in your browser

IX.P – Poetry HTML Template

IX.Q – Poetry HTML file viewed in your browser

Step 10 –

Familiarise yourself with your Template in Notepad++

Scroll down to where you see:

> Place Your TV/Film Script Title Here, or

> Place Your Play's Title Here, or

> Title of Your Novel Goes Here, or

> Title of Your Poetry Book Goes Here: and

> Replace this with your own title

Then go to:

> Your Author Name Goes Here, or

> by Author Name Here, or

> Author Name: and

> Replace with your name

Memorida: Replace black text –

The text shown in black on all four of the eBook interior HTML templates, is notifying you where to place your own manuscript – read it carefully and replace my text with your own – copying and pasting the HTML paragraphs into the order that you so require

CAUTION: Take care when inserting your own text – do not delete or change any of the coding as the formatting will be removed and your file will show errors

Memorida: Save to gain –

After you make any changes to the template, always click Save, followed by Refresh in your browser, otherwise alterations will not appear

Step 11 – (For NOVELS)!!

Insert your Chapter Titles into Template using Notepad++

Scroll further down, you will notice Chapter 1. If you have chapter names instead of numbers, replace Chapter 1 with your chapter title

The template consists of two example chapters – you will need to copy and paste these until to have the right amount of chapters you require following Chapter 2 – if you do not have subtitles, remove the example line along with its coding before and after

Step 12 – (For NOVELS)!!
Insert Chapter 1's First Line into Template using Notepad++

Where you see: This is the first paragraph of your chapter ... replace this with the first line of your Chapter 1. This paragraph is formatted without indent

Step 13 – (For NOVELS)!!
Insert the Rest of Chapter 1 into Template using Notepad++

Where you see the line: <p>Copy and paste the parts of this template to suit your requirements ...</p> replace this with the rest of your Chapter 1

Memorida: Decoding paragraphs –
<p> and </p> are the opening and closing codes
for each paragraph

Step 14 – (For NOVELS)!!
Insert Paragraph Coding to the Rest of your Chapter 1 whilst in Notepad ++

> Highlight all your paragraphs in Chapter 1, (excluding paragraph 1), from paragraph 2 and onwards, then
> Press Ctrl + H to activate pop up box Find and Replace
> Ensure Regular Expression is chosen (located bottom left), and
> Type the following text:
> Find what: ^(.+)$
> Replace with: <p>$1</p>

> Click Replace All (see picture IX.R)

IX.R

Note-This: Now when you view all your paragraphs in Chapter 1, you will have a <p> at the forefront and </p> at the end – each paragraph is indented

Step 15 –
Replication

Repeat the procedure of Step 14 for every one of your novel's chapters

Step 16 –

With Reference to the Steps of this Chapter ...

Now apply your new skills to the back matter of your eBook, such as Copyright and Acknowledgements sections ...

B
L
O
G

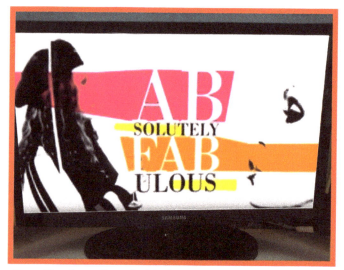

Jennifer Saunders (Eddie) & Joanna Lumley (Patsy)

**Opening titles to
BBC TV situation comedy series
Absolutely Fabulous
(2011-2012 specials)**
Pictures taken by IB whilst watching televison

Joanna Lumley (Patsy)

Finding your inner "Patsy" is an Ab Fab way to write better fiction

Bolly banter

Patsy has a strong identity: big hair, fast-living, ready-wit, this she practices every day (as a writer take heart from this) practicing an identity everyday can help craft your writing voice ==> Remember: hone the voice; iron out imperfections

Absolute agelessness

Patsy doesn't allow age to hold her back, in fact she can't locate her birth-date; and in much the same way, writers can acquire a freedom from age ==> Remember: age doesn't come into it - all a writer needs is a healthy imagination and self-discipline to script words

During the cocktail hour

Pasty keeps an awareness to what's new but if it doesn't suit her, she let's it go! So faze out the phase; spare yourself from temporary writing fashionistas, unless it benefits you ==> Remember: don't feel obliged to write new literary genres; write your way and allow this to carry you forward

Pasty Stone is a fictional character on BBC TV series Absolutely Fabulous, portrayed by actress Joanna Lumley. Series creator: Jennifer Saunders, who plays the lead role of Edina Monsoon

The 12 COMMANDMENTS of an AUTHORPRENEUR

Demographics

#9

Thou shalt NOT

approach companies to sell
your books when their
customer demographics
don't match your own

New | ✓   🗑 Delete   📁 Archive   Junk | ✓   Sweep   Move to ✓   Categories ✓   •••

NS   Naomi Smith <Naomi@jojomamanbebe.co.uk>
Thu 01 03 10:26
You ✉

Dear Ida and Gwen,

Hope your week is going well.

Thank you for sending Laura a copy of 'The Bear Who Used Up All His Growls', it is a lovely book.

However it is too old for the JoJo demographic. We only really sell board books.

Thank you very much again for considering JoJo.

Kind regards,

Naomi

Naomi Smith
PA to Managing Director

JoJo Maman Bébé
Design, Buying & Marketing Office
JoJo House Cloisters Business Centre 8 Battersea Park Road London SW8 4BG
Tel +44 (0) 2076 226543
Mob +44 (0) 7976 923915

On the positive: Naomi Smith, PA to MD -
Laura Tenison MBE, described the book as "lovely"

Image above is a screenshot of actual email

Practicing writers do not create solely from their own imaginations,
but also the seeds of overheard conversations

10

Mistakes are opportunites in disguise
they offer scope to re-look at the situation
from a different point of view

- Eebygumologists, fictional creatures in book:
The Bear Who Used Up All His Growls
by ZB

Extract from Chapter 8 - author Zizzi Bonah

ALICE RETURNS
THROUGH THE LOOKING–GLASS

"Oh, yes," said Alice. "I think I have quite got into the habit of asking the ask instead of doing the do." Then reaching down to the dandelion clock, she said quite plainly, in case the dandelion clock was in any doubt to her meaning. "I will have to forcefully exhale on you, my dear. And the number of exhales it takes for all your hair to fly off your head and away on the breeze, will tell us the number of the time."

"For all the petals in Rosemead," protested the dandelion clock. "I have never know such obtrusive behaviour in all my life! If you knew about character-isation, you would know it is acted out through one's behaviour and desires, from the first to the last, in order to be believable."

"Here, here," said another dandelion clock just off by the thicket. "And overmore, if you intend to take the time where exactly do you plan on keeping it?"

"Now look here," said Alice to the second dandelion clock. "I have no argument with you."

"I should think not!" protested the second. "It is most rude to go around picking arguments with plant life when you haven't substantiated the present picking. And I maybe short-sighted, but even I can see you have no vase to place your pickings in."

266

Convert your eBook to ePub via Calibre

Calibre Calling

Question: What happened to the girl who never changed? Answer: She never changed anything

I am of the firm belief, a change is as good as a reply, likewise, you are going to change, or rather covert, with a little BIG help from Calibre

It is important to emphasise that all retailers and distributors allow eBooks to be uploaded as .ePubs, therefore you are going to convert your HTML file into an ePub file, here is how:

Step 1 –

Place your HTML file in Calibre:

> Open Calibre

> Go to Add Books (see picture X.A)

X.A – "Add Books" icon is the first on the left-hand side

> Select your HTML file (see picture X.B)

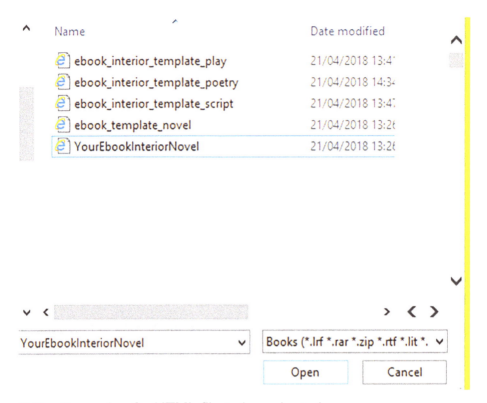

Name	Date modified
ebook_interior_template_play	21/04/2018 13:4
ebook_interior_template_poetry	21/04/2018 14:34
ebook_interior_template_script	21/04/2018 13:4
ebook_template_novel	21/04/2018 13:26
YourEbookInteriorNovel	21/04/2018 13:26

YourEbookInteriorNovel   Books (*.lrf *.rar *.zip *.rtf *.lit *.

Open   Cancel

X.B – Example of a HTML file to be selected

Step 2 –
Add Metadata to HTML file:

> Click Edit Metadata (at the right of Add Books – see picture X.A)

A pop up box will now be visible, fill in the following:

> Title: Your Book Title

> Title Sort: Your Book Title

> Author(s): Author Name

> Author Sort: Name, Author

> Comments: Your book's synopsis/short description

> Click Browse button to insert your eBook cover

> Click OK (see picture X.C)

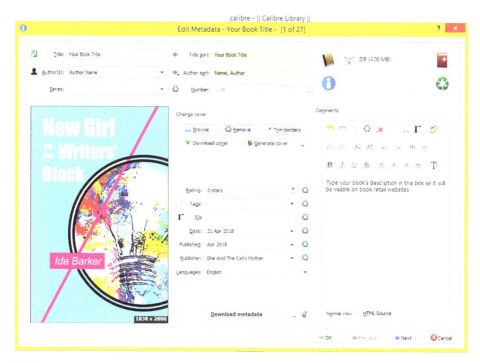

X.C

Step 3 –

Input Structures for your eBook file

before Converting:

> Click on your eBook in list so it becomes highlighted

> Click Convert Books (at right of Edit Metadata – see picture X.A)

> A pop up box will now appear

Select the eBook format you want to export to:

> Look at the top right corner – (see a dropdown menu)

> Select EPUB (see picture X.D)

X.D

> Look at the left side of your screen

> Choose Structure Detection

> Go to Chapter Mark

> Select None (see picture X.E)

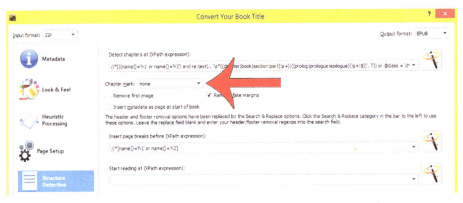

X.E

> Look at the left side of your screen

> Choose Table Of Contents

> Go to Level 1 TOC (XPath Expression); type the following text:
  //h:p[re:test(@class, "chapter", "i")] (see picture X.F)

> Tick box Manually Fine-Tune The TOC After Conversion Is Completed (see picture X.F)

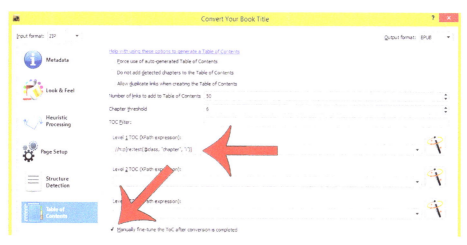

X.F

> Look at the left side of your screen

> Select EPUB Output

Tick boxes: (see picture X.G)

> Preserve Cover Aspect Ratio

> Insert Inline Table Of Contents

> Put Inserted Table Of Contents At The End Of The Book

> Click OK

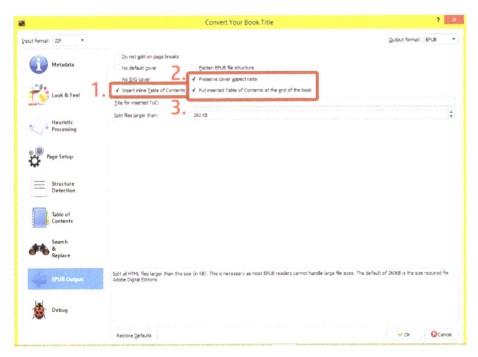

X.G

Note-This: The spinning wheel at the bottom right corner indicates Calibre is converting your HTML file into an ePub

Step 4 –

Review your Table of Contents

After a moment or two, a pop up box will appear, providing everything is displayed as you like it, click OK

However, if you see chapter sub-titles that you do not want visible, all you need do to remove them is:

> Click on the entry you do not want

> Select Remove This Entry

> (Repeat for any others you want removing), then

> Click OK (see picture X.H)

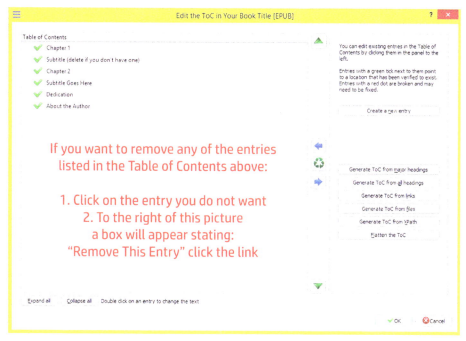

X.H

Step 5 –

Save your ePub file:

> Click Save To Disk – fourth from top right (see picture X.A)

> Choose the folder you want to save to on your computer

Step 6 –

Clarifying which File to Upload to Retailers/Distributors

In the folder that Calibre has processed, you will see many saved files – only one file is to be uploaded and that is the ePub file!! (see picture X.I)

X.I

Note-This: When uploading your ePub to IngramSpark, ensure you have renamed it YourISBN.ePub

Step 7 –

Upload your ePub to a Validator to Check Coding Errors:

> Go to: validator.idpf.org

> In the Choose File, locate your ePub file on your computer

> Press Validate (see picture X.J)

EPUB Validator (beta)

Submit an EPUB document for validation. Your file must be 10MB or less.

Choose File   No file chosen

1. Click on "Choose File" to upload your HTML eBook file

Validate

2. Once uploaded, Click on "Validate"

About this site

This site uses EpubCheck to provide validation information for EPUB 2 and 3 documents. If you are creating commercial EPUBs in volume, you must install EpubCheck instead of using this site.

Want to contribute? Go to https://github.com/IDPF/epubcheck/wiki/Contribute.

X.J

Note-This: After a few moments the Validator will inform you of any errors. Do NOT worry #GirlLikeYou!! So long as you have not deleted any of the necessary HTML coding on the downloaded template you will be tickerteeboo

Memorida: Correcting ePub errors –
In my early days of creating ePubs, I would have a
list of errors, these I would always fathom out with

277

the help of:

> Education Google

> One night's lost sleep

> A supply of tea, coffee and sweet cakes

I find everything is easier once you embrace it and become interested in the situation, as opposed to being deflated by it

Remember #GirlLikeYou – you will always learn more from one mistake than ever a collection of successes!!

.Be brave

.Be bold

.Believe in you

BLOG

"full of beans" Quentin Letts' praise

for Zizzi Bonah's paperback

Alice Returns Through The Looking-Glass: A Musical Vaudeville Stage Play

THE DAILY MAIL

Northcliffe House,
2 Derry Street,
Kensington,
London, W8 5TT

Gwen Hulgh and Ida Barker.

Harrogate
North Yorkshire

9 October 2017

October 2017

A MUSICAL VAUDEVILLE STAGE PLAY
By Zizzi Bonah

Alice Returns
Through The Looking-Glass

For children of all ages

STAGE PLAY

Dear ladies,

How kind of you to send me a copy of Zizzi Bonah's play script. At first glance it certainly looks to be full of beans.

Yours sincerely,

Quentin Letts.

Quotes of praise for your book

Displaying a quote of praise on your book cover should say something positive about the book and/or its author by someone other than yourself

Its aim is to action at least one of these points:
1. encourage the reader that this is the kind of book for them
2. give credence to this book
3. give credence to this book's author

Ultimately; it should pursuade the reader to buy the book

Praise should be sort from:
1. Well-known individuals (famous or experts in the same genre as book)
2. Media mentions (journalists or bloggers)
3. Customer reviews (sourced from amazon or goodreads)

You don't need a whole page full of praise, as some readers find multiple glowing words a put-off (knowing they are being sold-to). Instead choose one or two short, succinct, punchy phrases to capture their imagination; encouraging them to read on to your first page

The

12 COMMANDMENTS

of an

AUTHORPRENEUR

Quotes

#10

Thou shalt NOT

use un-authoritative quotes
to promote the quality of
your published book

"An excellent read"
Author's mother

"Outstanding!
I couldn't put this
book down"
Steph Fry from author's
local chip shop

"Fiction's new phenom"
Colleague from author's day job

zizziology.com

What's the saying? "Mum knows best"

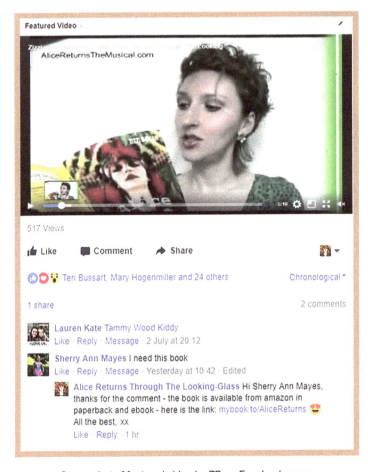

Screenshot of featured video by ZB on Facebook page

*Upload a video of yourself reading out
an extract from your book to help start
a dialogue with potential readers*

11

Some days are diamond; some days are stone

- Anon
a Yorkshire saying

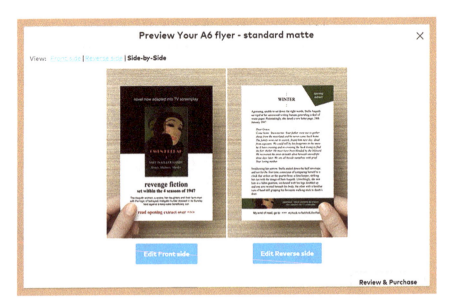

Screenshot of GH's book flyers; designed by She And The Cat's Mother; printed by vistaprint

Have you ordered flyers to spread the word of your book(s)?

Upload your paperback and eBook to distributors

Success: Only a Stone's Throw Away

Each retailer and distributor will inform you how to upload to their system with a one-step-at-a-time approach. I urge you to not rush but try to enjoy the process – within hours you will have a published book available to be bought worldwide

> *Memorida: How does my eBook look to buyers? – It is possible to preview your eBook by downloading a free ePub reader, such as Adobe Digital Editions. Alternatively, ask a friend to purchase your book in return for a coffee-shop outing, then view your eBook on their device (what are friends for ...)*

Note-This: Some people do not realise an eBook can be downloaded and read on any device, such as a computer, laptop, iPad or mobile phone – help spread the word that eBooks are not exclusive to eReaders!!

Congratulations #GirlLikeYou

You have now reached the end of the formatting knowing-how-to-know-do, but Donut Forget: with every ending, there is always a new beginning

Meet Change with Change

You have decided to change your situation by self-publishing, this will force people around you to change also, as there will be times when you are less socially available as you self-dedicate. The relationships that matter are those that allow you to grow – be your own best friend and do not give your dreams over to those who discourage you

www.GirlLikeYou.online

And, while you take time out to enjoy your moment of accomplishment, I hope the pages within this manual have encouraged, cheered and reassured a #GirlLikeYou not to stand still for long ... if you would like to recommend this book, post a review at the retailer you purchased it from

BLOG

SOUTH SANDS BRIDLINGTON

This is a postcard written to myself whilst a teenager

Bamforth
POST CARD

POST OFFICE
PREFERRED

To me in the future,

Robin's return, ambition to burn,
Mother tongue told you so.
Make your dreams reality,
Or life could be full of frugality.
    love from me in the past,
        ida Barker

5 012491 000167

Postcard home

A note to self that isn't a grocery list

We often write words of encouragement to family and friends, but have you ever written to yourself?

Recently, I was reminded of a postcard home - written to my future self - while attempting to declutter; though something of a mistake to start reminising with possessions from the past, as what should take no longer than a couple of hours, ends up taking the best part of your day ...

Result:
Best intentions go to waste, you don't throw anything out that may come in handy, therefore, nothing is thrown out!!

What might you write to your future self on a postcard home?

The 12 COMMANDMENTS of an AUTHORPRENEUR

Pronunciation

#11

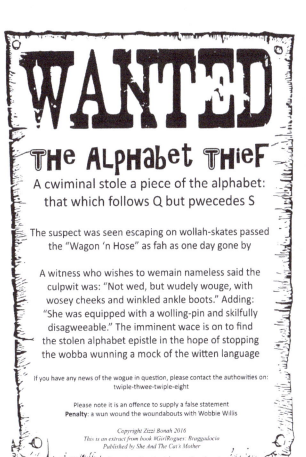

WANTED

THE ALPHABET THIEF

A cwiminal stole a piece of the alphabet:
that which follows Q but pwecedes S

The suspect was seen escaping on wollah-skates passed
the "Wagon 'n Hose" as fah as one day gone by

A witness who wishes to wemain nameless said the
culpwit was: "Not wed, but wudely wouge, with
wosey cheeks and winkled ankle boots." Adding:
"She was equipped with a wolling-pin and skilfully
disagweeable." The imminent wace is on to find
the stolen alphabet epistle in the hope of stopping
the wobba wunning a mock of the witten language

If you have any news of the wogue in question, please contact the authowities on:
twiple-thwee-twiple-eight

Please note it is an offence to supply a false statement
Penalty: a wun wound the woundabouts with Wobbie Willis

Copyright Zizzi Bonah 2016
This is an extract from book #GirlRogues: Braggadocio
Published by She And The Cat's Mother

One out of three isn't bad!

*The above verse was inspired by the pronunciations of TV host <u>Jonathan Ross</u>
who speaks his R's as W's*

Torquay big wheel & IB 2013: pictures taken by IB and GH

You're on high, reaching the
furthest point: Chapter 12

12

When people ask me if I went to film school I tell them, 'No, I went to films.'

- *Quentin Tarantino*
film director/writer/actor

And finally ...

Use the following pages to write down your notes: websites of interest, action plans and joined up thinking. The best way to gain momentum in this business is to write and publish another book – so don't limit yourself to one. Keep on keeping on. There is a chance for a #GirlLikeYou, so receive it with both hands:

.**Take action**

.**Reinvent yourself**

.**Create your own opportunities**

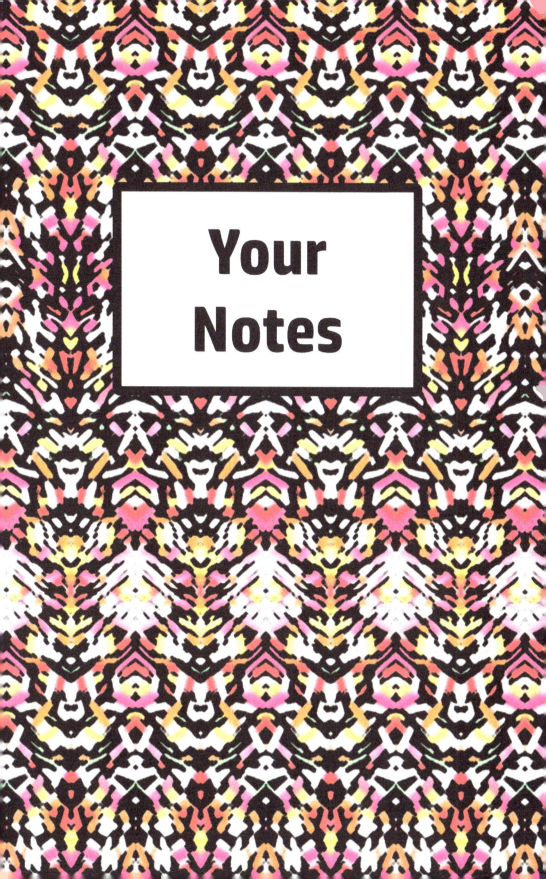

Your
Notes

Start a campaign with a hashtag and see where it leads you

Creating your own social media banners is a good way to share your message with others users

Nothing gets started unless someone starts it - You!

- GH

Visit
website and comment
on your experiences
of getting self-published
and help bring about a
`#GirlLikeYou` community,
whereby likeminded
authorpreneurs share their
ups and downs with
each other

www.GirlLikeYou.online

Paperbacks | eBooks | Audiobooks
by this publisher include:

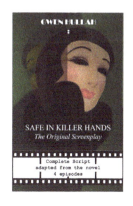

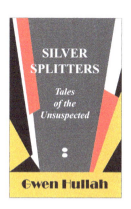

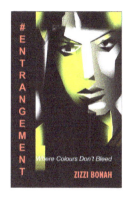

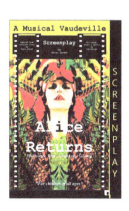

www.ingramcontent.com/pod-product-compliance
Lightning Source LLC
Chambersburg PA
CBHW052143070326
40689CB00051B/3181